The Home Sales Kit

Selling Your Own Home Made Easy

HOW TO AMERICA, INC.

ADAMS PUBLISHING
Holbrook, Massachusetts

Published by Adams Media Corporation
260 Center Street, Holbrook, MA 02343

ISBN: 1-55850-938-0

Printed in the United States of America

D E F G H I J

This publication is designed to provide accurate and authoritative information with regard to the subject matter covered. It is sold with the understanding that the publisher is not engaged in rendering legal, accounting, or other professional advice. If legal advice or other expert assistance is required, the services of a competent professional person should be sought.
— From a *Declaration of Principles* jointly adopted by a Committee of the American Bar Association and a Committee of Publishers and Associations

This book is available at quantity discounts for bulk purchases.
For information, call 1-800-872-5627 (in Massachusetts, 781-767-8100).

Visit our home page at http://www.adamsmedia.com

CONTENTS

Before you get started ...

HOW TO AMERICA, INC.

INTRODUCTION

When you bought this Home Sales Kit, you joined the millions of Americans who have challenged the status quo and saved themselves thousands of dollars in the process. We can't guarantee that selling your own home will be easy. . .or that you won't ultimately turn to a real estate agent for help. But the fact that millions of do-it-yourself home sellers have been successful tells you that you can be too — if you know what you're doing and follow our suggestions for success.

The purpose of this kit is to give you the advantage over those do-it-yourselfers who know they want to save money...but not much else, when it comes to selling their own homes.

It's not our intention to mislabel the real estate professional. As you will see in these chapters, real estate agents can be valuable allies to the self-seller; and if you are willing, they may even get a fair chance to make some money from your sale. If you do decide to exercise that option, however, the agent won't get to keep all the marbles for a change.

Remember this: The only difference between you and a professional real estate salesperson is knowledge. Like any profession, the real estate business has its small percentage of top performers. But the vast majority of the "pros" are mere workaday mortals who use a stock set of basic sales forms and systems to attract, sell, and close some sales. The most important of those procedures, plus many more, are contained in this kit. You can learn and execute these procedures the same way that a professional would in selling your home. The difference is that once your house sells, you leave lots more cash in your pocket for your new home purchase instead of paying out big bucks to a stranger.

You can do it.

Many non-sales professionals feel intimidated by the mysteries of making and closing a sale. They think they lack the insight, the know-how, the persuasive powers that they assume are the heart and soul of sales. But the fact is that many of the stereotypes of salesmanship are overdrawn exaggerations.

Selling is a simple, direct, time-honored ritual of one-on-one commerce. Regardless of how timid or reserved you may think yourself to be, the odds are that you have been an effective salesperson more than a few times in your life. In fact, you are probably selling things every day in your life–selling suggestions to your spouse, ideas in your workplace, opinions to your friends. You may not be peddling pots and pans or encyclopedias door to door, but you are bound to be selling something nearly all the time.

So much for the pep talk. It's time to get down to business.

A product that sells itself.

You have a distinct advantage over the sellers of many commodities less tangible than real estate, such as insurance, financial products, computer software, etc. That advantage is that you are selling the commodity that represents the prestigious pinnacle of the product chain; a home. There is no symbol more substantial, no product or investment considered more sound in American society than your home.

Second, there is a buyer for your home. You are proof of that. You bought the home yourself, and that means that others who share similar tastes and physical requirements will likewise be attracted to your home. The home will sell; the questions are simply when, for how much, and to whom. The condition of your community, along with your capacities for diligence and patience, will provide the answers to most of those questions.

To the right buyer your home will largely sell itself. Certainly you'll need to help the sale along as best you can with your own variety of gentle persuasion, but the sale of a home requires none of the hard-sell tactics associated with buying a car or with high-pressure insurance sales. If your buyers like what they see, they will be your best salespeople.

The savings stakes are high.

Rather than charging a flat fee for their services, real estate agents have historically worked on a commission basis. Over the years, the real estate industry has standardized the fee for the sale of residential homes at 6-7% of the selling price. While the prevailing tradition in your market may vary, the commission on the sale of new construction homes is often 1% less,

HOW TO AMERICA, INC.

and the commission on residential lots or other bare land tracts are approximately 10%. Commissions on the sale of commercial buildings are usually in the vicinity of 5%.

Obviously, the commission of greatest interest to you right now is the one charged for homes–because that's how much extra money you will have if you sell your home yourself. The other commission rates were noted above to help illustrate a point; that all real estate commissions are, by their nature, arbitrarily set fees that may in no way accurately reflect the amount of time or effort expended by an agent in selling a piece of property. In fact, if you took the average 6-7% residential sales commission and divided it by the number of hours a given real estate agent spent on a given sale–you would probably come up with an hourly pay scale that would boggle the mind.

You know real estate agents represent many homes for sale; have many "listings," and therefore spread small amounts of their time among many other sellers in the market place at any given time.

But the real estate commission's potential to provide extraordinary hourly compensation can be turned to the seller's advantage–when the seller gets to keep the commission.

Let's say you devote 20 hours of labor, plus $500 to $1,000 in advertising and legal costs to the sale of your home that would have cost you a $4,000-5,000 commission if sold through an agent. Even after subtracting advertising costs, that still can add up to a net hourly rate of $75 to $200 per hour for your trouble!

The thousands of dollars that you save by selling yourself is not just "mad money" that you can splurge in celebration–it is a substantial chunk of wealth that you can use for improvements of your next home, a retirement fund, the education of your children, or any number of other responsible functions.

The larger real estate markets have a Multiple Listing Services (MLS) that consolidate all current houses for sale into a regularly updated book (about the size of your yellow pages phone book) that contains pictures and vital statistics on each home for sale in the market. Some agents allow their buying clients to look through the MLS book and pick out homes that are of interest. The agent then arranges inspections of the homes that appear most appealing to the prospects. The real estate agent is merely acting as a finder in the home selection process–helping the buyers find a home they like–just as you will in selling your own home. Even with professionals, there is very little "salesmanship" involved…just the persistence and patience that are the keys to any thorough sales process.

NOTES:

COMMISSION TABLE OF SAVINGS

The savings that you will realize by selling your own home are quite easy to compute using the table below. Simply multiply the normal commission for the sale of a home in your market by the dollar amount of your asking or actual sales price. The example below is based on a $100,000 sales price.

$100,000 sales price
x   7% commission
$ 7,000 in savings to the seller

Remember that most agents try to get a 10% commission on the sale of bare land...and remember that agents are often negotiable on the commissions they charge.

The below chart indicates the amount of commission money you can save per $10,000 of your selling price.

Commission rate	Savings per $10,000	Savings per $50,000
10%	$1,000	$5,000
7%	700	3,500
6%	600	3,000
5%	500	2,500
4%	400	2,000
3%	300	1,500
2%	200	1,000
1%	100	500

How much am I going to save in commissions?

$ _____   (Your approximate home value)
x (6) (7)   (Commission 6% – 7%)
$ _____   **(Your approximate dollar savings)**

HOW TO AMERICA, INC.

NOTES:

Your motivation advantage.

When you list your home for sale with a real estate agent, you are making a big commitment. You are signing a legally binding contract that obligates you to pay a sales commission when your home sells–regardless of who sells it. We've all heard the tales of woe from sellers who became frustrated with the lack of results from their agent…started running ads of their own…and ended up selling their own homes on which they still had to pay a 6-7% commission! As unfair as that may seem, it is a too-often repeated fact of life. You owe it to yourself to try selling your home yourself first, using this kit, rather than trying it out of exasperation after you've listed your house and know that you'll still owe a commission even if you sell your own home.

Lastly, remember this: no matter how skilled or successful a professional real estate agent is, he or she can't match your motivation to sell your own home. Even though the agent's 7% stake in selling your home is considerable, you have a 93% majority interest in the sale. As a self-seller, your stake in the sale is even higher at 100%, giving you the most motivation of all.

Just because you expect to save a lot of money by selling your own home is no reason to splurge on home improvements. Pace your upgrading budget carefully. Prioritize those improvements that will be the most obvious, and most impressive to buyers. Remember that the purpose of any improvement is not the fulfillment of "pride of ownership," but rather strictly utilitarian; namely, to help you make a faster sale.

Selling a home is like panning for gold. Somewhere in all that slurry are the shiny nuggets you're looking for. There's bound to be some disappointment and fatigue between the creek and the assay office, but if you stick with it, you will be richly rewarded for your efforts.

HOW TO AMERICA, INC.

Preparing your home

PREPARING YOUR HOME

The irony of selling homes through real estate agents has always been the idea that after just a few accumulated hours of work, an agent walks off with 6-7% of your cash; the dollars you have spent years accumulating with mortgage, maintenance, and tax payments–not to mention the immeasurable elbow grease spent in your home and yard–that made the market price possible. Let's face it: as the center of our existence, our homes consume more of our income, time, and TLC than any other component of our lives. This is a fair deal, because while we take it for granted, quality shelter is the most important asset in our lives. For these and other reasons, the time and money that we invest in our homes over the years is well spent…but that doesn't mean that you should have to share it with real estate agents when it comes time to sell.

When you list your home with a real estate agent, it will still be you–not the agent–who will be required to get the home ready for showings to prospects. When listing the home, the agent will be full of suggestions about how your home should be spruced up to show better. But after those courteous suggestions are made, the agent will drive away–leaving you to do the work. We're not trying to suggest that real estate agents should be expected to make improvements to the homes that they list. We're merely suggesting that you deserve to be compensated for your home improvements.

Once again, there are no secrets to getting your home ready to present its first and best impression. Most of the things that should be done are common sense. Yet you'd be surprised how many sellers, in the excitement and pressure of their home sales process, tend to overlook some of the most critical home preparation necessities.

The following is a checklist of the priority items that need to be taken care of in order to give your home its top eye appeal, its best chance of selling as fast as possible, and at your price.

Neatness.

This is the most basic of the basic preparations. A clean, orderly, uncluttered appearance can make up for a multitude of other problems in the home. Clutter can make large houses seem small and small houses seem like cracker-boxes. Clutter is one of the greatest enemies for the home seller.

The solution to the clutter problem is simple: get rid of it. Everything from magazine racks to closets to your garage and basement should appear to have plenty of unused open space. Even in smaller homes, a lack of clutter creates a convincing sense of spaciousness. Kitchens and closets are especially important issues. Both must be clean, orderly, and blessed with wide open space. Clean the attic so it is neat and has space available. Take extra clothes and cooking utensils over to Aunt Minnie's if you have to, but don't let them kill your sale with the evil of clutter.

Do an objective, discriminating inspection of your home's other cosmetic features. Walls should be cleaned or repainted in neutral tones…windows and fireplaces should be clean…woodwork nicks filled with color-matched putty sticks (you can buy these at any home improvement store)…and the whole house should be dusted, vacuumed and cobwebs removed (remember corners of ceilings and window casings). Be sure all lighting works, inside and out. A well lit home shows well.

Pay special attention to bathrooms. Eliminate any mold and stains in the shower, tub, medicine chest, sinks, and toilets and replace worn or stained toilet seats–they are a surefire turn-off for fastidious prospects. Check the caulking around sinks, tubs, and showers.

In the yard, make sure that flower beds and lawns are neatly edged and free of debris. Hedges should be trimmed, and thick, light-blocking foliage should be thinned around windows to allow more light into the home. It's always a good idea to plant some colorful flowers, especially in the front yard, if the season permits. And of course, any refuse strewn around the yard should be removed.

As we said at the start, the basics are the most important things to take care of in order to maximize your home's marketability. Some people go overboard in this sense by expecting extensive and expensive home improvements to sweep buyers off their feet. The truth is that statistically, most structural home improvements such as added bedrooms, bathrooms, swimming pools, and workshops don't begin to pay for

HOW TO AMERICA, INC.

themselves in terms of the value they can add to the sales price of a home; they are generally of value only for your own convenience and enjoyment.

The addition of new rooms is even less feasible from a fiscal recovery standpoint. Instead, make the most of the home you have now. And if it is necessary for you to spend a little extra money to bring your place up to snuff, you'll feel better about doing it when you remember all the real estate commission money you're saving by selling yourself.

NOTES:

CHECKLIST OF THINGS TO REMEMBER WHEN GETTING YOUR HOME READY

☐ Make sure the entrance to your home is clean and pleasant from curb to front door; including a neat lawn, and a well-painted door.

☐ See that all of your home's most visible surfaces are pleasantly painted or wallpapered.

☐ Keep drapes open to maximize the amount of natural light in the home.

☐ Wash all windows inside and out.

☐ Have all light fixtures working properly, including those in closets.

☐ Repair any leaky faucets and remove any rust stains in sinks or tubs.

☐ Eliminate undue clutter from all storage areas such as closets, attic, and basement.

☐ Pay special attention to bathrooms. Remove mildew stains and repair any loose, crumbling caulk or grout around tile and tub areas.

☐ Keep all bedrooms orderly and inviting with attractive furnishings, wall hangings, and bedding.

☐ Keep pets out of the way when visitors are expected, and remove any pet stains or lingering odors. This is very important.

☐ Fix any faulty kitchen appliances and sticky cupboard doors or drawers.

- -

NOTES:

HOW TO AMERICA, INC.

CHECKLIST FOR SPECIFIC HOME IMPROVEMENT

EXTERIOR

- ☐ Storm windows.

- ☐ Foundation cracks.

- ☐ Foundation vents – make sure all are intact and clean.

- ☐ Masonry chimneys – re-mortar loose bricks.

- ☐ Roof – remove debris, nail down loose shingles.

- ☐ Gutters – repair holes and any separations from eaves.

- ☐ Downspouts – paint over any rust spots or streaks. Make sure they are connected at top & bottom.

- ☐ Windows – check for loose caulk and chipped paint, broken or cracked windows..

- ☐ Porches – seal cracks and remove any standing water if concrete. If wood, secure loose railings and stain or paint as necessary.

- ☐ Insects and vermin – better that you discover and remove them than your buyer. Look for telltale bore holes and droppings in all wooded areas of the house as well as underneath.

- ☐ Make sure all outdoor lighting works.

- ☐ Trim overgrown shrubs and have all landscaping in top condition.

- ☐ Plant blooming flowers in flower beds if season permits.

- -

NOTES:

HOUSE EXTERIOR Need of Service	To Be Done	Supplies & Equip. Needed	Cost	To Be Done By	Date
Yes ☐ No ☐ painted recently					
☐ ☐ no blistering or peeling paint					
☐ ☐ shutters on straight					
☐ ☐ gutters, downspouts clean & clear					
☐ ☐ recently painted					
☐ ☐ exterior lights all working					
☐ ☐ turned-up shingles					
☐ ☐ exterior fixtures painted					
☐ ☐ chimney mortar tight					
☐ ☐ flashing secure, leak free and tight					
WINDOWS					
☐ ☐ cracked panes					
☐ ☐ sashes recently painted					
☐ ☐ work easily					
☐ ☐ caulking in good condition					
☐ ☐ clean					
PATIOS & TERRACES					
☐ ☐ surface smooth and clean					
☐ ☐ no standing water or moss					
☐ ☐ free for storage					
☐ ☐ If porch or terrace is wood, it should be recently:					
☐ ☐ stained or painted					
☐ ☐ free of termites or dry rot					
☐ ☐ railings sound and secure					
☐ ☐ only treated wood to be in direct contact with the ground					
LANDSCAPING & GROUNDS					
☐ ☐ LAWN					
☐ ☐ lawn condition good					
☐ ☐ grass mowed					
☐ ☐ edges trimmed					
☐ ☐ fences secure					
☐ ☐ trees trimmed to show the house					
☐ ☐ walks, clean no cracks or moss					
☐ ☐ driveway, clean no cracks or moss					
☐ ☐ planting beds, new bark dust, no weeds					
☐ ☐ TREES					
☐ ☐ dead limbs trimmed					
☐ ☐ dead trees removed					

HOW TO AMERICA, INC.

HOME SALES KIT™

Need of Service			To Be Done	Supplies & Equip. Needed	Cost	To Be Done	
Yes	No					By	Date
☐	☐	**FOUNDATION & PLANTINGS**					
☐	☐	shrubs trimmed to see the house					
☐	☐	dead shrubs removed					
☐	☐	dead shrubs replaced					
☐	☐	**DRIVEWAY**					
☐	☐	surface smooth					
☐	☐	holes patched					
☐	☐	asphalt recently sealed					
☐	☐	gravel smoothed and weeded					

NOTES:

HOW TO AMERICA, INC.

SPECIFIC HOME IMPROVEMENT CHECKLIST:

INTERIOR

☐ Have a pleasant assortment of plants and blooming flowers throughout the house.

☐ Make sure all light fixtures have bright, working bulbs.

☐ Wash all windows, inside and out.

☐ Clean all switchplates and wall areas around them – they tend to collect grime.

☐ Make sure doorbell works.

☐ Attractive paint or wallpaper on all walls.

☐ Have all wood or linoleum floors clean and freshly waxed.

☐ Have working lights in all closets.

☐ Have mailbox in good repair.

☐ See that all windows open easily.

☐ Oil any squeaky hinges.

☐ Make sure carpets are clean and secure. Have any loose carpet areas stretched tight and curling edges tacked down.

☐ Paint over any stain marks on ceiling or walls.

☐ Fill any gouges in woodwork with matching putty, and nail holes in wall with matching paint.

☐ Have furniture arranged to maximize a look of spaciousness in every room.

☐ Clean dust and dirt from all window sills.

☐ Eliminate any creaks in floors by driving finishing nails into creaky area (this can be done through carpet on covered floors too).

☐ Clean stove of all grime on the surface and under burner elements, and make sure oven is clean.

☐ Have the kitchen sink empty and clean.

☐ All cupboards should be carefully arranged to suggest ample space.

☐ Bathroom sinks, toilets, and tubs should be immaculate.

☐ Bathroom tile should be free of grime, loose grout and mildew.

HOW TO AMERICA, INC.

☐ Hang fresh towels in bathroom and kitchen.

☐ Eliminate any dripping faucets.

☐ Have all bathroom and kitchen counters free of clutter.

☐ Clean out bathroom medicine chests.

☐ Make sure the shower curtain is clean.

☐ All beds should be neatly made.

☐ Garage should be neat and free of oil stains; garage door should operate smoothly.

NOTES:

HOUSE INTERIOR Yes No DECORATING FLOWERS AND PLANTS	To Be Done	Supplies & Equip. Needed	Cost	To Be Done	
				By	Date
☐ ☐ interior flowers, bulbs, plants ready for use in:					
☐ ☐ entry hall					
☐ ☐ living room					
☐ ☐ kitchen					
☐ ☐ patio					
☐ ☐ other					
ENTRANCES					
☐ ☐ hall light working					
☐ ☐ light fixture clean					
☐ ☐ closet doors don't squeak					
☐ ☐ closet light working					
☐ ☐ closet not crowded					
☐ ☐ rugs and carpets clean					
☐ ☐ floors waxed					
☐ ☐ windows washed					
☐ ☐ curtains clean					
☐ ☐ entry lights working					
☐ ☐ entry light fixtures cleaned					
☐ ☐ mailbox recently painted or cleaned					
☐ ☐ door brass polished					
☐ ☐ doorbell working					
☐ ☐ steps structurally sound					
☐ ☐ if wood, free of rot					
☐ ☐ door recently painted or stained					
☐ ☐ woodwork recently painted or stained					
☐ ☐ door hardware working					
FAMILY ROOM					
☐ ☐ wallpaper secure to walls					
☐ ☐ walls clean or recently painted					
☐ ☐ windows washed					
☐ ☐ cracked or broken panes replaced					
☐ ☐ curtains clean					
☐ ☐ window sills clean					
☐ ☐ woodwork recently painted, or stained					
☐ ☐ floor recently cleaned					
☐ ☐ carpets clean, tacked down					
☐ ☐ door hardware works					
☐ ☐ furniture placed to best show room size					

NOTES:

Need of Service Yes No	To Be Done	Supplies & Equip. Needed	Cost	To Be Done	
				By	Date
LIVING ROOM					
☐ ☐ wallpaper secure to walls					
☐ ☐ walls clean or recently painted					
☐ ☐ windows washed					
☐ ☐ cracked or broken panes replaced					
☐ ☐ curtains clean					
☐ ☐ window sills clean					
☐ ☐ woodwork recently painted or stained					
☐ ☐ floor recently cleaned					
☐ ☐ carpets clean, tacked down					
☐ ☐ door hardware works					
☐ ☐ furniture placed to best show room size					
DINING ROOM					
☐ ☐ wallpaper secure to walls					
☐ ☐ walls clean or recently painted					
☐ ☐ windows washed					
☐ ☐ cracked or broken panes replaced					
☐ ☐ curtains clean					
☐ ☐ window sills clean					
☐ ☐ woodwork recently painted or stained					
☐ ☐ floor recently cleaned					
☐ ☐ carpets clean, tacked down					
☐ ☐ door hardware works					
☐ ☐ furniture placed to best show room size					
KITCHEN					
☐ ☐ pantry neat					
☐ ☐ sink free, clean and no leaks					
☐ ☐ appliances all work					
☐ ☐ unexpired warranty and operating manuals available					
☐ ☐ range, hood, filter, and ventilator free of accumulated grease and odors					
☐ ☐ cupboards:					
☐ ☐ free for excess storage					
☐ ☐ arranged orderly					
☐ ☐ counters free of clutter					

NOTES:

Need of Service Yes No	Item to Be Done	Supplies & Equip. Needed	Cost	To Be Done By	Date
BATHROOM #1					
☐ ☐ replace loose or broken tiles					
☐ ☐ caulk joints, where necessary					
☐ ☐ brush grime from joints					
☐ ☐ leaky faucets repaired					
☐ ☐ sink stains removed					
☐ ☐ counters clear					
☐ ☐ clean towels out					
☐ ☐ shower curtain clean, bright, fresh					
☐ ☐ peeling wallpaper repaired					
☐ ☐ walls washed or repainted					
☐ ☐ lights working					
☐ ☐ floor clean					
☐ ☐ drawer and cabinet hardware working					
BATHROOM #2					
☐ ☐ replace loose or broken tiles					
☐ ☐ caulk joints, where necessary					
☐ ☐ brush grime from joints					
☐ ☐ leaky faucets repaired					
☐ ☐ sink stains removed					
☐ ☐ counters clear					
☐ ☐ clean towels out					
☐ ☐ shower curtain clean, bright, fresh					
☐ ☐ peeling wallpaper repaired					
☐ ☐ walls washed or repainted					
☐ ☐ lights working					
☐ ☐ floor clean					
☐ ☐ drawer and cabinet hardware working					
BEDROOM #1					
☐ ☐ wallpaper secure to walls					
☐ ☐ walls clean, free of smudges					
☐ ☐ windows washed					
☐ ☐ cracked or broken panes replaced					
☐ ☐ curtains clean					
☐ ☐ window sills clean					
☐ ☐ woodwork recently painted or stained					
☐ ☐ floor recently cleaned					
☐ ☐ carpets clean, tacked down					
☐ ☐ door hardware works					
☐ ☐ furniture placed to best show room size					

NOTES:

HOW TO AMERICA, INC.

Need of Service			To Be Done	Supplies & Equip. Needed	Cost	To Be Done	
Yes	No					By	Date
BEDROOM #2							
☐	☐	wallpaper secure to walls					
☐	☐	walls clean, free of smudges					
☐	☐	windows washed					
☐	☐	cracked or broken panes replaced					
☐	☐	curtains clean					
☐	☐	window sills clean					
☐	☐	woodwork recently painted or stained					
☐	☐	floor recently cleaned					
☐	☐	carpets clean, tacked down					
☐	☐	door hardware works					
☐	☐	furniture placed to best show room size					
BEDROOM #3							
☐	☐	wallpaper secureto walls					
☐	☐	walls clean, free of smudges					
☐	☐	windows washed					
☐	☐	cracked or broken panes replaced					
☐	☐	curtains clean					
☐	☐	window sills clean					
☐	☐	woodwork recently painted or stained					
☐	☐	floor recently cleaned					
☐	☐	carpets clean, tacked down					
☐	☐	door hardware works					
☐	☐	furniture placed to best show room size					

NOTES:

Need of Service	To Be Done	Supplies & Equip. Needed	Cost	To Be Done	
Yes No				By	Date
BASEMENT					
☐ ☐ structural elements sound					
☐ ☐ no cracked wall or sagging beams					
☐ ☐ no dry rot					
☐ ☐ no termites					
☐ ☐ no water penetration					
☐ ☐ no dampness					
☐ ☐ no musty or sewer-gas odor					
☐ ☐ no stopped-up drains					
☐ ☐ have excess storage					
☐ ☐ clean condition					
☐ ☐ all lights working					
☐ ☐ Stairway:					
☐ ☐ free of storage					
☐ ☐ handrail secure & clean					
☐ ☐ lights bright and working					
☐ ☐ Furnace:					
☐ ☐ inspected, cleaned and filter changed.					
GARAGE					
☐ ☐ free of accumulated storage					
☐ ☐ recently swept and orderly, no oil stains					
☐ ☐ tools and equipment neatly stored					
☐ ☐ light fixtures working					
☐ ☐ door operates easily and quietly					
☐ ☐ electric door-opener works					

NOTES:

Pricing your home

PRICING YOUR HOME

The setting of price is the most crucial maneuver you will make in your campaign to sell your home. One of the greatest obstacles to realistic price-setting is an age-old phenomenon called pride of ownership. It's only natural that people grow attached to a home that they have devoted years to, just as we all become attached to favorite cars and other inanimate objects. But the risk in this case is that it's all too easy to allow your own love of your home to unrealistically influence its pricing. If pride of ownership deludes you into setting your price too high, you're in for a long wait and lots of disappointment... and you'll have only yourself to blame.

Get a second opinion.

The first thing you need to do when preparing to price your home is the same thing you'd do before undergoing major surgery–get a first and then the crucial second opinion. The best source of that opinion is the real world of the marketplace itself. You don't have to be a professional to find out what the professionals think about home prices in your neighborhood; all you have to do is pick up the phone.

There are several readily accessible sources you can use to help realistically price your home. Begin by looking in the classified ad section of your biggest local newspapers on the busiest days for real estate advertising–typically Saturdays and Sundays. Almost all newspapers categorize their real estate ads by location, so check the classification that includes the ads for homes in your immediate area.

Compare the vital statistics of the advertised homes in your area to those of your home; square footage, number of bedrooms and bathrooms, and other pertinent amenities. Look at the ads placed by real estate firms. Pay attention to the lingo used in the ads, such as the abbreviations that are often used to describe home features and financing, and note the points of interest that the pros focus on. It won't take long for you to absorb the techniques of writing ads for your home–and it takes even less time to determine the approximate range of prices that others are asking for homes similar to yours, in your area.

Don't be afraid to call on a few of the ads

describing homes that you find similar to yours, whether they are by professional agents or other self-sellers. Ask for more details about the homes, and then simply ask the advertisers point-blank if they're getting many calls on their ads. People are usually excited to share such innocent information if asked politely, and their input can be valuable to you. The sellers who report getting more calls are probably the ones with the prices that are most in tune with the true market in your area.

In addition to the newspaper ads, call real estate agents directly for their input. Let them be your tutors for a "crash course" in real estate in your area. Ask them such questions as the state of the home-selling market in your area... which lenders have the best mortgage terms...and which newspapers they would advertise in if they were given the listing on your house (these, of course, are the newspapers you should plan to advertise in). If agents actually come to your home, say during an open house, invite them to offer suggestions on improvements or changes that should be made to make a quicker sale. There is really no harm, however, in being honest with agents; you're likely to get more information from them by laying your cards on the table. Tell them that you are considering selling your home, and that you're not sure what homes like yours are selling for in your neighborhood.

How to use "comps".

Any real estate agent will be more than happy to compile a list of "comparables" or "comps"– descriptions of a group of homes that are for sale or that have been sold recently that closely compare to yours. This list will be invaluable to you in your determination of a sensible sales price.

Keep in mind that a real estate agent will develop a "comp" list for you for one reason only–and that is to get a listing for his sale of your home. If agents that you approach with a "comp" request knew you were a self-seller, you can be sure that they wouldn't be so forthcoming with their assistance, if indeed they'd be willing to help you at all.

Are you being unscrupulous by asking an agent to provide you with comps for your home without revealing that you plan to sell it yourself? No. In fact, you may be doing the

agent a big favor, and we'll explain why in the next chapter. For now, the message is that agents are an excellent yardstick with which to accurately measure your home's value, and thereby save you sales time. They work in real estate every day, and who should know better than a real estate agent the price that you should actually be able to command for your home.

Beware of "Optimist's Inflation".

A word of caution, though; make sure you ask your agent contact for comps of homes in your area that have actually <u>sold</u> as well as those still for sale. This is an important distinction. The spread between asking prices and actual selling prices can vary widely from one market to another, depending on local conditions. You should know how wide the spread between asking and selling prices is in your area.

Remember, too, that agents often tend to overestimate a home's value as an enticement to get the seller to list with them. Remind yourself to allow for a little "optimist's inflation" on suggested sales prices that you solicit from agents.

Before you start spending money on the promotion of your house for sale, you deserve to know whether you'll be paying to promote pie in the sky or money in the bank. Unrealistic optimism can be contagious; sometimes entire neighborhoods suffer sluggish home sales because everyone is kidding themselves about the strength of their market, or they are too proud to lower their prices to a realistic level. As a self-seller, though, you will be spending your own dollars to sell your home—not a real estate brokerage's dollars—so it is essential that you pick a price your market will respond to.

How to use title and escrow companies.

Another convenient source of sales prices for homes in your area are local title insurance and escrow companies. Many people don't realize what a convenient and economical source of information these firms can be.

In most states title insurance companies serve as one of the most vital links in the real estate machine. Among their principal services are "title searches" to verify for buyers that the title to property being purchased is free of liens, delinquent taxes, or other obligations that the seller might not be aware of.

Title companies also insure the status of

titles to buyers and lenders involved in purchasing and lending on real estate, and the title company is liable if any undetected title problems surface after a sale or real estate loan is closed. In many states, title insurance companies handle the paperwork, transaction recording, and other administrative details of closing real estate sales, all for a nominal fee. (Don't worry—as a self-seller, you will benefit from these services also).

People are surprised that title insurance companies can furnish complete details about a property when given nothing more than that property's address. A property's physical dimensions, building size, taxes, assessed value, and most recent sales price are almost always available upon virtually anyone's request. Many title insurance companies still provide this valuable information service free, while others have begun to make a nominal charge. Real estate agents have relied upon the generosity of title insurance companies for years to develop leads and comps for clients, all with the understanding that the more title insurance companies helped agents, the more agents would be able to generate new business for the title insurance companies.

If you are unsure about the realism of your price, you're better off on the slightly higher side than the lower side. That's because if you price too low, you may gain an immediate sale but lose thousands of dollars. You can always lower the price if you seem to be getting little or no response.

Establishing market prices for real estate involves, at its best, more than a little guesswork. Even the values determined by professional appraisers often deviate thousands of dollars for the same property.

The Appraiser Option.

If you really want to be sure about the fair market value of your home before you start trying to sell it, you may want to consider having it professionally appraised. Appraisers are estimators of the "official" value of properties, that are used by lenders to structure the terms of real estate loans. Appraisers will use objective, businesslike techniques to arrive at a reliable estimate of price. If you decide to use appraisals, expect to pay $200 to $400 or more, and wait several weeks for the results. Also, don't expect any appraisal that you initiate for

HOW TO AMERICA, INC.

your home to be accepted by your buyer's lender. Many lenders insist upon selecting their own appraisers to evaluate a property before they will commit loan money to a buyer.

Appraisers will in some cases do a less expensive "Opinion of Value" evaluation for you that, at $75 to $100, is significantly cheaper than a full-blown appraisal. If your home is worth $100,000 or less, you may want to require that your appraiser is FHA-approved, since you may end up selling to a buyer who plans to purchase with FHA financing. To further reassure yourself as to the reliability of your appraiser, you should select from a pool of appraisers who belong to such accredited professional organizations as the Society of Real Estate Appraisers or the National Association of Independent Fee Appraisers.

Once you have solid comps collected from the newspaper, real estate agents, title companies or an appraiser, you are armed with the best tools you can have when entering the real estate market–reality. You will then know not just what some neighbor, friend, or agent says your home is worth, but what you <u>know</u> it should be worth in today's true market.

Now it is safe to inject some subjectivity into the price-setting process. How motivated are you to make a quick sale? If you are being transferred, or have immediate financial needs, you may want to come in under the average asking price...not <u>sales</u> price. . of the related comps in your area. If you are in no rush, you can afford to hold out for a higher price.

Consider the other factors in your local real estate market. Have real estate loan interest rates been moving up or down recently? Higher loan rates typically dampen the home sales market; lower rates create more activity. How is the economy in your area? How high is employment; how low is unemployment? And, are you willing to carry a contract on part of the balance that will be owed on your home? (See chapter on land sales contracts.) If you help your buyer finance the purchase of your home, you should hold out for a higher price as compensation for your financing help.

When setting your price, also take into account those elements of the sales effort that are tax deductible. **Consult with an accountant** to get a full rundown on current tax deductibility, but here are some of the costs that have been considered deductible when cost are offset against gain:

- Advertising costs
- Regulations permit the seller to enjoy tax benefits for improvements made to make a property more marketable if such improvements are made within the 90 days prior to a sale, and/or paid for within 30 days following the date of sale.
- Legal fees
- Recording fees
- Inspection fees (if the seller agrees to pay these)
- Any loan costs borne by the seller such as points (one point equals 1% of the amount borrowed; these are charged by some lenders)
- Sales commissions, if you allow agents to become involved
- Sellers 55 years or older should be aware of the once-per-lifetime capital gains exemption. If the property being sold has been used as a principal residence for an accumulated total of three years out of the five years prior to the sale, the 55-year or older seller is allowed to exclude up to $125,000 in capital gains from that sale from that year's reported income.

Save the comps you've accumulated–they can double as effective sales tools for the marketing of your home (more on that in the next chapter). And remember that if your price turns out to be high, you can always lower it. People do it every day. But as a self-seller, you have a built-in advantage over the others. It's better to be facing the possibility that you may not get your full price than the certainty that you'll pay a commission, even after lowering your price from listing value.

EXPENSE FORM

Use the following expense form to keep track of all the expenses related to your sale.
It will come in handy at tax time.

Repair or improvement	Cost	Date Billed	Date Paid
Advertising			
Legal fees			
Recording fees			
Inspection fees			
Commission or consulting fees			
Name			
Address			
The For Sale by Owner Home Sales Kit™			
Total			

THE <u>UNRELIABLE</u> EYE
Your HOUSE as seen by...

Your Lender   Yourself

Your Buyer   Your Appraiser

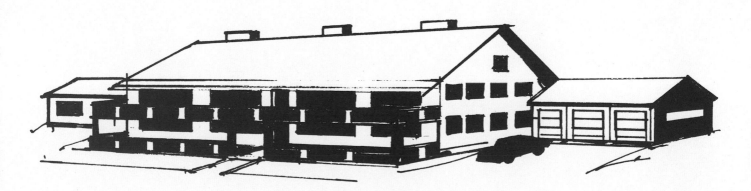

Your Tax Assessor

CHECKLIST FOR SETTING YOUR HOME'S PRICE

☐   Go into homes for sale in your neighborhood similar to yours for comparison.

☐   Be aware of the minimum price you're willing to accept.

☐   Add a "buffer" in anticipation of buyer negotiation.

☐   Get at least three real estate agents' opinions of your home's value in writing. Save the material from Comps to use in the Marketing Chapter.

☐   Check classified newspaper sections to find current market prices for homes in your area similar to yours.

☐   Be sure you don't overprice.

☐   If you're not satisfied with your own ability to determine a market price, hire an appraiser.

- -

NOTES:

HOW TO AMERICA, INC.

Competitive Market Information

Your Address _____ Date _____

For Sale Now: Address/Nbrhood	Bed-rooms	Baths	Fam Rm.	F/P	Approx. Sq. Ft.	Asking Price	Days on Mkt.	Terms	Remarks
_____									
_____									
_____									
_____									

Sold Past 12 Months: Address/Nbrhood	Bed-rooms	Baths	Fam Rm.	F/P	Approx. Sq. Ft.	Asking Price	Days on Mkt.	Date Sold	Sales Price	Terms	Remarks
_____											
_____											
_____											
_____											

Espired Past 12 Months: Address/Nbrhood	Bed-rooms	Baths	Fam Rm.	F/P	Approx. Sq. Ft.	Asking Price	Days on Mkt.	Terms	Remarks
_____									
_____									
_____									
_____									

NOTES:

HOME SALES KIT

HOW TO AMERICA, INC.

Sales from Multiple Listing

In these spaces, affix information on related properties that **have sold** in your area that you receive from real estate agents. Then, show this sheet to your propects to justify your home's asking price, but do so only if the comparable prices reflect favorably on your asking price.

①   ②

③   ④

HOW TO AMERICA, INC.

Homes Presently on the Market from Multiple Listing

In these spaces, affix information on related properties that **have sold** in your area that you receive from real estate agents. Then, show this sheet to your propects to justify your home's asking price, but do so only if the comparable prices reflect favorably on your asking price.

①   ②

③   ④

HOW TO AMERICA, INC.

Marketing your home

MARKETING YOUR HOME

The key word for the self-seller is patience. Selling your home takes time even in the hottest real estate markets. There may well be times when you have to buoy your spirits by reminding yourself that worthy things are worth waiting for. If that doesn't work, try reminding yourself of all the commission money you're going to save by sticking it out and selling yourself.

Before you start devoting full energy to selling your home, you need to decide <u>when</u> the time is best for you to mount your campaign. Seasonal factors are very important in home selling, and timing shouldn't be ignored. Spring and summer are the obvious best home selling seasons. The fall, especially after school starts and with holidays approaching, is a historically slow period. It is surprising to learn that many real estate pros consider January to be as big a sales time as some of the peak summer months. In general, though, the warmer weather and "new beginnings" sentiments of spring signal the start of the season for home selling that's likely to be about as good as it can get.

Once you've decided when to start selling, the next order of business will be posting "For Sale" signs on your front lawn. The signs should be clearly visible to traffic going both directions in front of your house, and should be positioned so that they will not be blocked by parked cars.

Avoid amateurish, homemade signs. They can be your worst enemy. A large preprinted or professionally painted sign will send the right message about your property, and fairly sing out the attributes you most want to highlight: value, neatness, and professionalism. Most sellers don't think they have to front the costs for a sharp-looking sign—and that's a major mistake. By making sure you've put your best face forward, you will eliminate the negative reactions.

Once you have the sign situation comfortably in control, it's time to get the word out. Begin right in your neighborhood, using one of the oldest and most reliable tricks in the real estate professional's bag.

Every neighborhood has at least one person who is heavily involved in the area's culture and is surprisingly knowledgeable about the lives of other neighbors in the area. Basically, that is a diplomatic description of what is more commonly referred to as a "busybody."

Actually, the word "busybody" carries an unfair stigma. The fact is that neighbors of this description are among the most reliable good Samaritans and crime stoppers you can find. In many ways, their neighborhood is their life; they simply enjoy knowing what's going on in the world around them.

If you haven't already, develop a rapport with your neighborhood's busybody. Even if you haven't been close with this person before, take the initiative to introduce yourself, and explain that you're about to begin efforts to sell your home. In the interest of being a good neighbor, say you wanted to notify your neighbors of your intentions first. That way, if they know of any friends or relatives who happen to be looking for a home, they can be the first to spread the word and pass around the opportunity to help sell your home. What could be more neighborly than offering your neighbors the opportunity to have a hand in choosing their new neighbors, rather than gambling on the strangers that you might otherwise sell to?

In all likelihood, your neighborhood activist will quickly set the grapevine buzzing with your interesting news. As another respectful gesture, offer to host a "sneak preview" open house for your neighbors. This simple gesture just might be the one that sells your home—it has certainly been effective in many sales. To help spread the word, give your friends and neighbors the home sales leaflets that you have prepared to advertise your home.

Leaflets

Leaflets can be printed cheaply and easily at any quick-print shop. A sample and a form are enclosed with this kit. You don't have to be a professional to produce a professional-looking leaflet. It should have a well-taken clear black and white photo of your home dominating the top of the page. Make sure the photo shows your home's best outside features. If you feel that your photo is not good enough to show your home's "best side," consider having a local artist do a rendering of the house, instead. You can find such artists in the Yellow Pages, or through real estate firms in your area. Artists have the advantage of illusion that a camera doesn't enjoy; they can portray your home with flattering

flair. If street appeal is a problem with your house, don't hesitate to give this option a try; it's not that expensive, $20 - $30, and it could attract far more prospects than a weak photo will.

Below the photo at the top of your leaflet, feature your home selling price and highlights in a concise, clean looking layout. Basic points to be included are total square footage, number of bedrooms and baths, fireplaces (how many and if they are brick), the distance to elementary, intermediate, and high schools, a description of the garage (how many cars, if there's extra space for workshop), type of heating (be sure to list air conditioning if you have it), details about your utility room if there is one, property taxes, and any other information that is likely to distinguish your home and make a positive impression.

Beyond the basics, you should capitalize on any of the "extras" that your home may offer. Are there hardwood floors? A swimming pool, either in-ground or above ground? A large yard or special landscaping? Ornate mantles, energy-efficient fireplace inserts, or woodstoves? Extra storage areas? If your home is especially energy efficient, be sure to highlight that highly desirable feature, even to the point of specifying the amount of your average monthly heating cost if it is impressively low.

At the bottom of your flyer, be sure to include the address of your home, and phone numbers where you can be reached during the day, night, and weekends. You must make yourself accessible at all times, because you never know which call will be _that_ call.

Have your quickie print shop run off several hundred copies of your flyer. They're cheap, and you're going to distribute plenty of them–to the point of overkill. First, give a dozen or so to the neighborhood busybody that you've already so trustingly "taken into your confidence." Next, blitz all the other neighbors with copies on the doorsteps, either tucked under a mat or behind a screen door so they won't blow away. (it is illegal to insert such a notice in mailboxes.)

Depending on how serious you are, you may want to more broadly circulate your flyers by leaving them in laundromats, in the windows or on the counters of grocery stores that give you permission to do so, on public bulletin boards in supermarkets, churches, beauty parlors and anywhere else that it strikes your fancy to staple, stick, or send one.

You may even want to have your kids (or hire some) put your leaflets under the windshield wipers of cars parked in the lots of movie theaters, malls, or anywhere else that affords a concentration of cars, provided such a means of advertising is legal in your community (check with your local police department or city hall).

Don't restrict the distribution of your leaflets to your immediate area, either. Give them exposure all over town if you can. Call the relocation departments of your city's largest employers, and the personnel departments of colleges, hospitals, etc. Offer to send them leaflets describing your home to help them find desirable housing for their transferees into your area. This is another source of leads frequently tapped by real estate professionals. To heighten the interest of your contacts in these departments, offer an enticing referral fee if they send you a prospect that ends up buying your home–say even $600. You'd be surprised how quickly relocation people will take a keen personal interest in the sale of your home when there's something in it for them.

NOTES:

AD HEADLINE HERE...

PHOTO OF YOUR HOME HERE

ADDRESS: 0123 ANYWHERE U.S.A.   PRICE: $150,000

NEIGHBORHOOD: BEAUTIFUL U.S.A.

APPROX SQ. FT.: 2500   AGE: 02   STYLE: Contemporary

BEDROOMS: 4   BATHS: 3   HEAT: Gas

ROOF: Shake   LOT SIZE: 10,000   FIREPLACE: 2   GARAGE: Double

SPECIAL FEATURES:

- Floor Plan (indicate guest house, split bedrooms, etc.)
- Deciding factors (pool, dining room, other "must haves")
- Location (cul-de-sac, "walk to's," golf course, etc.)
- Architecture (style, construction, builder)
- Amenities (fireplace, vaulted ceilings, decorating touches)
- Existing financing (PITI, amount; indicate assumable)
- Potential financing (buy-down, trade)
- Down payment (initial investment)
- Association fee
- Directions or map for secluded properties

SCHOOLS: GRADE_____ MIDDLE_____ HI_____

TAXES: $1,500_____ OWNERS NAME_____

PHONES: DAY_____

EVE_____

Information above is from sources deemed reliable, but is not guaranteed.

ADDRESS:_____ PRICE:_____

NEIGHBORHOOD:_____

APPROX SQ. FT.:_____   AGE: ___   STYLE:_____

BEDROOMS: ___   BATHS:__   HEAT:_____

ROOF:_____   LOT SIZE:_____   FIREPLACE:__ GARAGE:_____
SPECIAL FEATURES:

SCHOOLS: GRADE_____ MIDDLE_____ HI_____

TAXES:_____ OWNERS NAME _____

PHONES: DAY_____

EVE_____

Information above is from sources deemed reliable, but is not guaranteed.

As a rule of thumb, be prepared to budget 1/2 to 1% of your sales price for advertising. When it comes to advertising, you must be prepared to bite the bullet and part willingly with a few dollars. Thrift is a marvelous principle to live by, but stinginess when it comes to advertising is a risky proposition. Advertising is the lifeblood of your sales effort...your direct link to buyers...and you must do justice to this powerful sales tool or risk costing yourself more time and money later.

Even if you've never written an ad in your life, take heart in the fact that successful ads are written every day by amateurs. Before you start trying to formulate the copy of the ad itself, ease into the task by listing the selling points about your home that you feel are most impressive. You are the most authoritative source on this subject; after all, you live there.

Now, next to each point listed, write down one or more positive things that you feel each point represents to a potential buyer. Next, rank these points in what you consider to be their order of importance. By following these basic steps, you will have developed the building blocks of your ad.

All you need to do now is assemble these blocks into an ad that is understandable and hopefully, persuasive. Ads for homes are never very long, so try writing various versions until you arrive at one that you feel particularly comfortable with. Just remember to assemble the building blocks of your ad in a logical ranking with the most important attributes appearing first.

Look at the other home ads in the paper, especially the ones written by the professionals. Their ad-writing techniques are practiced and proven, so when in doubt, you can emulate their style with confidence. Use the enclosed checklists for effective ad writing.

Examples of ads will be found further on in this chapter.

NOTES:

CHECKLIST FOR WRITING A GOOD AD

☐ Look at ads for homes in your papers to learn how others – especially professional agents – write their ads for homes.

☐ List the ten most positive things about your home; then use them.

☐ Develop a selection of attention-getting headlines.

☐ Be aware of your home's vital statistics other than number of bedrooms and baths: such as total square footage, location of nearest schools, churches, bus lines, and other community features.

☐ Write the elements of your ad in order of importance.

☐ Emphasize any features or desirable financing that your home may have.

☐ Mention any open houses that you hold at the beginning of the ad – include the hours the home will be open, as well as the address and direction if it's a hard to find location.

☐ Specify number of bedrooms and baths early in the ad.

☐ Disclose the home's approximate location (Neighborhood).

☐ Consider a theme of urgency in the ad – such as "Transfer Forces Sale" or "Must Sell By (Date)" to generate more interest.

☐ Request a headline type size larger than the body copy of the ad – it will help the ad stand out.

☐ Prominently feature price if it is particularly attractive.

☐ Don't use confusing abbreviations just to save space.

☐ Advertise on the most effective days of the week (this should always include the weekend).

☐ Check on special repeat rates; some papers allow discounts of as much as 75% for ads that are repeated.

☐ Don't overlook regional, as well as city newspapers as effective advertising vehicles.

- -

NOTES:

THE KEY ELEMENTS THAT MAKE YOUR AD WORK

Research shows that buyers rank a home's features in the following order of importance:

1. Location of home 70%
2. Spaciousness 45%
3. Price and terms of financing 40%
4. Quality of construction 33%
5. Visual appeal of home 20%
6. Age of home 17%
7. Form of heating 17%
8. Basement 8%
9. Size of home's property 6%
10. Other home amenities 4%

Keeping the above priorities in mind, build your ad with the following proven ingredients:
1. A catchy headline (if you're holding an Open House, it should be announced at the top of the ad).
2. A hook – something special about your home related to price, location, financing, etc., that will grab interest and lead the reader further into the ad.
3. The meat – this is the main body of the ad and should contain all the pertinent facts about your home and what makes it special, presented in accordance with the above ranking of buyer priorities.
4. The call for action – your phone numbers, and the price of the home.

Pick the right day

As a home-seller, your favorite day of the week should quickly become Sunday. That's traditionally the best day for ad respons, and certainly a top day for buyer touring as well. It often costs more to advertise in Sunday papers because they are a premium advertising medium, but the nominal extra charge should be worth the extra exposure you will gain. An intriguing side benefit of weekend advertising is the "Sunday hangover," a phenomenon of calls that come in later in the week following a Sunday ad. This occurs because buyers who recreate on the weekend will often save their Sunday ads to follow up on later. This effect lends even more justification for the higher rates you may have to pay for a Sunday ad.

If your ad doesn't produce results, don't give up. Probe for weak points in your copy if it needs it, but above all, don't stop advertising. Try running ads on other days of the week, and try other newspapers or "for sale by owner" publications in your area.

How to handle agents

Once you start advertising, it's virtually a safe bet that you'll get calls from real estate agents interested in listing your home. As a matter of principle, some self-sellers are adamant in their exclusion of agents. They just can't bring themselves to pay any portion of a sales price to an agent, let alone a full 7%.

Such complete discrimination against agents can, however, be more damaging to you than to the agents told to get lost. If told to, they will get lost, while they could be helping you sell your house for a fraction of their usual fee instead. Let us explain.

We recommend that when agents call to solicit a listing, be polite. Explain that your objective is to avoid paying a full commission, but that if they're willing to accept one half or less of their normal commission on your home's sale, you'd be pleased to work with them. (This is assuming that you'd be willing to pay 2% – 3 1/2% of your sales price to an agent who could produce a buyer for you.)

Some agents will work on an adjusted commission basis, but beware. The next thing they're likely to tell you is that even if they work on a reduced commission, they'll still need a listing agreement with you that makes them your exclusive sales agent. Patiently repeat that you are more than willing to allow them some commission if they produce a buyer, but that you can't be constrained by any kind of listing arrangement, since you have no way of anticipating where your buyer will ultimately come from. This will separate the most ambitious agents from the less aggressive ones. Agents who have enough confidence in their own selling ability and enough appreciation for a fair opportunity to make a percentage of your home's value are the ones you'll hear back from. Unfortunately, many agents will refuse to work with such genuine opportunities, unless they are securely sewn up with a listing agreement that would pay them a commission regardless of who made the sale, and defeat the whole premise of you saving by selling yourself.

One way that agents can protect themselves when exposing prospects to your home is with

HOW TO AMERICA, INC.

what is called a one-party listing. This involves a form signed by the seller attesting that a single buyer, one party–by name, is to be exclusively listed to the broker/agent willing to show your home to that prospect. If an agent asks you to sign a one-party listing, and if you are willing to pay some portion of a commission which you and the agent have negotiated, then you have little to lose by signing a one-party agreement. Refer to our list of questions to ask real estate agents for more ideas.

Be persistent

In summary, then, selling your own home will demand consistent and diverse efforts from you. Get your signs in the yard, your flyers dispersed in the community, and your ads in the paper. Don't be afraid to take out the relatively cheap ads available in the "For Sale By Owner" publications available in most markets of reasonable size.

And most importantly, when ads are running, **stay by the phone.** This is one of the hardest things for some people to do, but you must discipline yourself because this is the crux of your entire sales effort. After going to the trouble of listing day, night, and weekend phone numbers, you must plan to be available at those numbers. If being away from the phone is unavoidable, use a telephone answering machine or answering service, as a backup. They're not that expensive, although you'll find that many people calling on ads will refuse to leave a message.

NOTES:

HOW TO AMERICA, INC.

SAMPLE LETTER TO SEND TO LOCAL REAL ESTATE AGENTS

Here is an example of a letter that you may want to formulate in order to inform local agents of your willingness to work with them on the sale of your home on a reduced commission basis.

(date)

Courtesy to Brokers

We are about to begin efforts to sell our home at (address), and we are not opposed to working with real estate agents. We are willing to conduct all showings of our home, finance all advertising expenses, and be responsible for all closing details. If you are interested in cooperating with us, we ask that you simply let us know the name and telephone number of any prospect of yours that you think may have interest in our home. We will then initiate contact with your prospect and handle everything from that point on.

If the prospect you refer to us ends up buying our home, we will pay you ___% of the sales price at closing. Your payment will be set up and assured through (name of escrow or title company, lawyer, or other credible entity). That's all there is to it.

(Here, offer a brief summary of your home's strongest selling points). We think our home is a quality value, especially at the reasonable price that we are asking for it. We welcome any questions you may have about our home. Please feel free to call us, or have your prospects call us at (phone number). We look forward to working with you.

Sincerely,

NOTE: Staple leaflet to your letter. In most cases each brokers office has mail slots for each agent. Call each office in your area, ask the secretary how many agents they have – go to each office and put in each agents mail boxes or give this information to their secretary to put in their mail slots.

How to handle callers

Be positive with callers. First, try to get callers to come by for a personal look-see. Try to counter every negative point that prospects might raise with gentle, but sure rebuttals. Besides being knowledgeable about your home's surrounding area–where the nearest schools, churches, shopping areas and day care centers are–also be conversant on the financing options available to buyers. Know what the most competitive rates available are for 30- and 15-year mortgages, for fixed rate as well as adjustable rate mortgages (ARMs). Build up current information from lenders and ask other pertinent facts about their loans, such as loan fees, and the time taken to process each loan. Rate information is also often in the Sunday newspaper business and/or home sections.

Your time spent gaining knowledge, will be time well spent, since many of your callers will be first timers; completely unfamiliar with the particulars of home buying, even though they are earnest, qualified buyers. To maximize your chance of selling to such buyers, you must serve not just as a seller, but as a consultant and confidant. **Give truthful information**, and be sure to offer to send each caller a flyer on your home.

The objective is to steer as many of your callers as possible toward visiting your home. The more traffic you can generate, the higher the odds will be that you make a faster sale. It is better to slightly oversell than to hold back and lose a prospect who will turn out to be a winner for someone else.

Open houses and showing your home

On weekends, it's a good idea to hold open houses. These make sense because you'll be home waiting for ad calls anyway. You may as well capitalize on the traffic driving by your home by putting a large "open" sign by or on the "For Sale" signs in your yard. If you do plan to hold an open house, announce in it your ad. Many buyers prefer to treat home buying like a shopping trip, and love to spice their weekends with home tour itineraries.

Obviously, many of these "tourists" will be nothing more than curiosity seekers. But in the gold-panning exercise that is home selling, you must be willing to endure a little idle chatter in exchange for the big payoff you'll receive on closing day.

When you do get prospects to tour your house, try to make them feel as much at home as possible. Two favorite professional tricks are to have the aroma of freshly baked cookies or bread wafting through the house, and have a fire burning in the fireplace or woodstove.

Map out a tour of your home that you think will show off its most flattering highlights, and then try to get your prospect to adhere to that controlled tour. If prospects stray, don't be too pushy or controlling. Try to end the tour in a comfortable area of your home, such as by a crackling fireplace in winter or a cool porch in summer. If things appear to be clicking between you and the buyer, offer a drink (soft, hot or otherwise) to add to the comfortableness of the moment.

Maximize your odds of making a good impression by having some professional touches on hand, like plat maps of your home's area that highlight the closest schools, bus stops, stores, and churches; a brief summary of the loan packages offered by local lenders; and, of course, the flyer you have prepared describing your home. Some people take a special interest in the location of the nearest police and fire stations, so it would be a good idea to be familiar with those as well.

During open houses or tours by appointment, have all drapes pulled open to allow as much light in as possible. Daytime appointments are preferable for the creation of positive first impressions.

Things to avoid during tours are: the lingering scent of unpleasant cooking or pet aromas, noisy children, intrusive pets, and above all, messiness.

However you do get people to visit your home, make sure that you always take names and phone numbers of those who stop by. You will want to stay in touch with all of your prospects with regularity. Any buyers who come to your home are almost certain to be touring others as well. They are likely to be in an intense home-hunting mode, and they could choose to make a selection at any time. So call your interested parties every few days–don't lose track of them. Ask if there are any further questions you can answer. Be a pest, but a courteous, caring pest.

Above all, keep at it and keep the faith. Those are words that every successful salesman lives by, and they can work wonders for you too.

HOW TO AMERICA, INC.

CHECKLIST OF HOME SALES STEPS

☐   Have a good photo taken or rendering drawn of your home.

☐   Set a realistic price.

☐   Prepare a leaflet with your home's picture and vital statistics.

☐   Research the best newspapers in the area to place ads in.

☐   Prepare an effective ad.

☐   Put your For Sale signs in an easily visible yard location.

☐   Distribute leaflets over a wide neighborhood area.

☐   Complete any necessary home repairs and improvements.

☐   Hold open houses on weekends, with Open House signs in the yard and down the street.

☐   Take names and phone numbers of all prospects who visit your home. (Use guest log we have provided for you).

☐   Have a lawyer review any earnest money agreements written before you sign.

☐   Have a lender work up sample monthly payments and loan fee costs that relate to your home's price. (See example included in qualifying buyer chapter.)

☐   Have an escrow or title company develop approximate closing costs for your sale. (See move-in cost form in qualifying your buyer chapter.)

☐   Have a lawyer review all closing documents prior to closing.

- -

NOTES:

Home Operational Expense Form

<table>
<tr><td colspan="2">FOR SALE BY OWNER
Home Sales Kit™</td><td colspan="7">OWNER:_____
ADDRESS:_____
RES. PHONE:_____
BUS. PHONE:_____</td></tr>
</table>

Month	Elec.	Gas	Water	Sewer	Refuse	Landscape	Assoc. Fee	
Jan.								
Feb.								
Mar.								
Apr.								
May								
June								
July								
Aug.								
Sept.								
Oct.								
Nov.								
Dec.								
Total								
Av. Mo.								

NOTES:

NOTE: Your buyer in most cases is going to ask for utility and other expenses associated with the operational cost of your home.

Property Information Sheet

LOT SIZE _____ X _____ VIEW _____

YARD: _____

FENCING: _____ GARDEN AREA: _____

RV PARKING: _____ PATIO/PORCHES: _____

DRIVEWAY: _____ SIDEWALKS AND CURBS: _____

OTHER: _____

ZONING RESTRICTIONS: _____

PROPERTY INFORMATION

OWNER: _____

OWNER'S ADDRESS: _____

TELEPHONE: _____ (res) _____ (bus)

PROPERTY ADDRESS: _____

LEGAL DESCRIPTION: _____

TAX ACCOUNT NUMBER: _____

ZONING: _____ USAGE: _____

TAX VALUATION:	TRUE CASH	ASSESSED
YEAR _____		
IMPROVEMENTS	$ _____	$ _____
LAND	$ _____	$ _____
TAX AMOUNT:	$ _____	$ _____

SCHOOLS: GRADE _____

            JR. HIGH _____

            SR. HIGH _____

            PAROCHIAL _____

CITY BUS: _____ (from property)

SCHOOL BUS: _____ (from property)

NEAREST GROCERY STORE: _____ (from property)

NEAREST SHOPPING CTR.: _____ (from property)

HOW TO AMERICA, INC.

Home Exterior Information Form

STYLE: _____

TYPE OF CONSTRUCTION: _____

AGE: _____ ROOF TYPE: _____ AGE: _____

SQUARE FOOTAGE:

    TOTAL : _____

    MAIN FLOOR: _____

    UPPER FLOOR: _____

    LOWER FLOOR: _____

    BASEMENT: _____

    USUABLE ATTIC SPACE: _____

GARAGE: _____ cars: _____ attached: _____ detached: _____

GARAGE DOOR OPENER: _____ INSULATION: _____

ENGINEERING

HEATING: _____ type: _____ fuel

FIREPLACE: _____

SEWER: _____ SEPTIC: _____ CESSPOOL: _____

WATER: _____ HEAT PUMP: _____

AIR CONDITIONING: _____

AIR CLEANER: _____ HUMIDIFIER: _____

WATER COMPANY: _____

ELECTRIC COMPANY: _____

TELEPHONE COMPANY: _____

GAS COMPANY: _____

NOTES:

Home Interior Information Form

AREA	DIMENSIONS	REMARKS
ENTRY	_____	_____
LIVING ROOM	_____	_____
DINING ROOM	_____	_____
KITCHEN	_____	_____
FAMILY ROOM	_____	_____
BRKF. NOOK	_____	_____
REC. ROOM	_____	_____
DEN	_____	_____
UTILITY ROOM	_____	_____
LOFT	_____	_____
MST. BEDROOM	_____	_____
BEDROOM	_____	_____
BEDROOM	_____	_____
BEDROOM	_____	_____
BATH	_____	_____
BATH	_____	_____
BATH	_____	_____
BUILT-INS	_____	_____

APPLIANCES INCLUDED IN SALES PRICE

RANGE _____	OVEN _____
HOOD AND FAN _____	MICROWAVE _____
REFRIGERATOR _____	GARBAGE DIS. _____
DISHWASHER _____	SMOKE DETECTOR _____
CENTRAL VAC _____	FOOD CENTER _____
TRASH COMPACTOR _____	FREEZER _____
INTERCOM _____	ALARM _____
WASHER _____	DRYER _____
SPA _____	SAUNA _____
OTHER _____	OTHER _____

SOME SAMPLE ADS FOR STARTERS:

Middle Aged Beauty
For Sale By Owner. She has had a face lift. New roof, new kit, new carpets, & 3 lg bedrooms. Located in lovely Downtown. $89,500. Call Day's xxx-xxxx; Eves xxx-xxxx (No Agents - Optional)

For Sale By Owner
Need a Playroom for the cookie crumbliers & Dad? Roomy ranch w/view, heated bsmt w/playroom & shop. 3 bdrm, 2 baths located in quiet nbhood. Only $125,000 Call Day's xxx-xxxx Eves xxx-xxxx (No Agents - Optional)

Wanna Cuddle?
This cozy charmer is for you. 2 bdrms, fenced backyard in area of nice homes. Close to everything. Clean & sparkling. Cute too! $25,950. Call Bill, Day's xxx-xxxx Eves xxx-xxxx

Remember Grandma's
Warm spacious Old charm on heights. 3+ bdrms, 2 baths, fam. rm, bsmt, eating bar in kitchen w-lots of cupboards, patio doors in fam rm. $195,000. Call Day's xxx-xxxx Eves xxx-xxxx

Plop Plop Fizz Fizz
Oh what a relief it is... to finally find your cape cod with 3 bdrm, fam rm, alum. siding, storm windows, new nook & remod. bath only, $36,000. Call Day's xxx-xxxx Eves xxx-xxxx

Little Dollhouse
Sparkling inside and out. Easy to heat 2 bdrm, toolshed w/storage, fenced back yd close in SW Bus service. Like new home. Don't miss this charmer! $85,000. Call Day's xxx-xxxx Eves xxx-xxxx

NOTES:

WORDS TOO LONG OR CANNOT BE ABBREVIATED

Assumable	Everything
Excellent	Buildable
Beautiful	Improvements
Financing	Landscaping
Features	Atmosphere
Spacious	Courts
Finishing	Opportunity
Seclusion	Over
Residential	Modern
Outstanding	Shopping

WORDS OVERUSED OR IN POOR TASTE

Prestigious	Divorce
Desperate	Features
Anxious	Amenities
Beautiful	Fantastic
Tremendous (not size)	Luscious
Widow	

CLASSIFIED ADVERTISING "BLOOPERS"

"Vaulted ceilings with build in appliances"
"Bachelor pad or secluded living. Walk to Bridlemile grade school"
"Living room with fireplace, with fold-out bed"
"Must sell: corner rock fireplace & front of home"
"Stone wall-to-wall floors"
"Double garage included"
"This home is on 85' x 89' lot" (trailer home)

SUGGESTED DESCRIPTIVE WORDS FOR YOUR AD

Home Design
rambling	wrap around decks
stunning	Cape Cod
one-of-a-kind	Victorian
vaulted ceilings	contemporary
cathedral ceilings	tri-level
open beamed	colonial
split level	ranch style
sunken	contempo ranch
	condo

Spaciousness

mammoth	vast
massive	ample
expansive	palatial
immense	rambling (ranch)

Condition

perfect condition	prime
precision maintained	top notch
A-1	needs TLC
impeccable	needs love
mint	elbow grease
move-in condition	bring your paintbrush
trim	roll out the drop cloth
immaculate	roll up your sleeves
apple pie order	challenge
spotless	easily expandable
squeaky clean	easy conversion to

Construction

quality	solidly built
fortress-built	sturdy
built like a fortress	meticulous
custom built	

Country

recluse	woodsy
retreat	small town
hermite	down home
hibernate	rural
tranquil	secluded
woody	rural accents

Decor

tasteful	tantalizing
professional	elegant
luxurious	quietly elegant
colorful	sensitive
with a flair	exquisite
zesty	opulent

Family Room

play room	dance studio
party room	sitting room
big-party-sized-room	intimate conversation room
recreation room	garden room
rumpus room	solarium
billiard room	studio
game room	den library
band practice room	exercise room
musician's corner	hobby room

Fireplace

massive	used brick
floor-to-ceiling	Old Dutch
fieldstone	Inglenook
cultured stone	full-wall fireplace
stucco stone	for roasting chestnuts

Landscaping

park-like	lush
trim	rich
manicured	towering trees
tropical	

Kitchen

gourmet	breakfast nook
epicurean	bright
country	cheery
dream	

Area

established prestige	near shopping
well located	easy access to
coveted	creekside
easy walk to	secluded
close-in	perfect privacy
near parks	private
near schools	

Porch

veranda	sundeck
sun porch	inner court
patio	courtyard
piazza	patio
gallery	portal
lanai	terraces
atrium	open gallery

Pool

sparkling	freeform
gem-set	for serious swimmers
stunning	country club
sunny	woodland setting
sun-lit	perfect pool site
glowing in warm spring sunshine	

Quiet Words

sedate (a sedate ranch)	quiet
subtle	restful
understated (elegance)	nest

HOW TO AMERICA, INC.

HOME SALES KIT ™

Small

compact	love nest
practical	honeymooners'
sensible	intimate
cozy	romantic
homey	storybook
lovers' retreat	doll-house

Sun

drenched in sunlight	sun-kist
natural light	sun-gilded knoll
sunny	sun-filled
sunlit	bathed in light
sunstruck	sun-swept hill
well-lit	sun washed
sun-warmed	sun-shiney

Verbs

interweaves (interwoven)	features
complements (sets off)	blends, combines
boasts	melds
featuring	possesses

View

superb	sensational
unlimited	mesmerizing
breath-taking	peaceful
exquisite	gorgeous
unparalleled	commanding
exceptional	unsurpassed
incredible	unforgettable
incomparable	sweeping miles-wide
spellbinding	far-reaching
fantastic	distant
fabulous	ethereal
striking	wooded
stunning	tree-top view
360	overlooking
magnificent	of lawn
panoramic	Bay View
panorama	Hills View
spectacular	vistas
an ever changing panorama	

Workshop

hobby shop
craft corner
potting shed

ADVERTISING ABBREVIATIONS

These should be avoided when possible, but here is a list of abbreviations that are easily enough understood to warrant judicious use in your ads.

fireplace	frplc
basement	bsmnt
daylight	dalite
living room	LR
family room	FR
master bedroom	mstr bdrm
refrigerator	refrig
possible	poss
contract	cntrct
payment	paymt
district	dist
square foot	sq ft
wall to wall	w-w
kitchen	kit
downtown	dwntn
utility	util
available	avail
large	lrg
condition	cond
assumption	assum
immediate	immed
built-in	blt in
garage	gar
minutes	mins
yard	yd

Adjectives for Ads

quaint	doll-house	irresistible
charming	cheerful	gracious
distinguished	special	handsome
prestige	stately	ornate
tantalizing	delightful	comfortable
captivating	refreshing	engaging
intriguing	enticing	ideal
tasteful	sleek	classic
elegant	magnificent	sumptuous
luxurious	enchanting	comfy
inviting	welcoming	pleasant
attractive	graceful	spectacular
distinctive	imaginative	dignified
attractive	smooth	sophisticated
prestigious	elegance	magnificence
elaborate	luxury	lavish
imposing	superb	smashing
sparkling	resplendent	extraordinary

Phrases

magnificently executed
proven design
timeless styling
state of the art
designed for tomorrow
tomorrow's design
now people
idea house
pace-setters choose
innovative new look
fluid floor plan
surprise extras
abundance of light (storage)
usable space
generous rooms (spaces)
wide open expansiveness
rambling rancher
space to spare, space to share
maximum convenience, comfort
artfully remodeled
pride of ownership
T.L.C. (tender loving care)
a bit of work will bring it up to date,
but a steal at yesterday's price
highly flexible (design, floor plan)
livability
sets an easy pace
easy-to-live-in
suits your life style
easy-to-love
reflecting the ease of the
California lifestyle
designed with little people in mind
room to grow
designed for hospitality
delight the eye
hard to match
true intrinsic appeal
aroma of new wood
candlelight and wine
variegated hues of
a perfect complement to
surrounded by the interior warmth of
wide range of
subtle emphasis
accented with
drawing on
handcrafted in wood
attention to detail
fine detailing
bright and cheery (breezy, airy)

right and bright
soul stirring contemporary
time-tested Western Ranch House
sharing its architectural heritage
the ground-hugging silhouette of
the Western Ranch
heavy-scale beams
on a generous scale
blissful bi-level
captivating effect
walls of glass
an architectural study
harmonious medley of
richly colored
rugged simplicity
rugged and austere
interplay of (planes, light, textures)
subtly, carefully designed
handsomely contrasted
the good life
down to earth
quiet revolution
demand excellence
express yourself
irresistible invitation
an invitation to
waiting to steal your heart
honeymooners haven
perfect for the indoor gardener
hanging plants love the
see it now while the roses bloom!
labyrinth of riding trails
equestrian setting
viewed from the sheltered seclusion of
tall cypress guards the entrance
what a place to come home to!
framed by aging shade trees
savor the privacy of
you'll see green from every window
your own enchanted garden
seek the solace of
veritable oasis
atmosphere of tranquility
cloaked in the privacy of
watch Spring approach from
mini-estate
mini-park
mini-kingdom
relished extra touches of yesterday
in the timeless tradition of
the charm of yesteryear
charm reminiscent of

reminiscent of Merry Old England
a bit of history can be yours
reflections of days long ago
with the patina of age mellowing
every line
exudes the rich aura of tradition
Mom-pleasing kitchen
farm kitchen with pantry
country kitchen
an "everybody ends up in the kitchen" kitchen
dining terrace
bewitching black bottomed pool
the chimney's ready for Santa,
the house is ready for you
bikers and joggers
city close but country quiet
location makes the price
twice as nice
quiet going no where street

this caring community
liberating mode of living (condominiums)
condominium craze
dollar-stretching duo
"rocking chair veranda"
ageless beauty
interesting architectural features
strong geometric lines
meticulously pieced together
creatively designed
added dimensions
indescribably intriguing
vintage material and craftsmanship
blend in perfect harmony
masterful craftsmanship
extra touch of elegance
unity and interest
creates interest
creates shining interest
unique theme thoughtfully planned

NOTES:

BASIC RULES FOR HOME SHOWINGS

☐ Emphasize the spaciousness of individual rooms.

☐ Make sure rooms are neat so they will look spacious.

☐ Make sure the sidewalks, landscaping, and porch leading to your front door make an attractive, orderly first impression.

☐ Fix any leaky faucets and scrub clean any sink or tub discoloration.

☐ Keep closets uncluttered and roomy looking.

☐ Have beds made, dresser tops straightened, and furniture neat in bedrooms. Avoid having clothes hampers visible in any bedroom.

☐ See that curtains are clean and unrumpled in all rooms.

☐ If during the day, have all curtains pulled open to maximize natural outdoor light. If at night, have all lights on.

☐ Provide adequate lighting in basements and attics and make each appear to offer plenty of unused storage space.

☐ Repaint any walls with worn or paint or wallpaper.

☐ Use a moist bar of soap to lubricate sticky doors and drawers or have them fixed permanently.

☐ Deodorize lingering pet or cooking aromas.

☐ Remove carpet stains.

☐ Have all landscaping looking neat and well manicured, with lawns cut short.

☐ Be knowledgeable about your home's area and its amenities and desirable features.

☐ Have a pre-planned home tour in mind that will accentuate the positives and minimize any negatives.

☐ Direct your discussion toward the prospect's strongest areas of interest; don't just try to sell, try to listen to your buyer's needs and respond to them.

☐ Don't oversell.

☐ Try to overcome every buyer's negative with a positive.

☐ Be patient and above all don't argue with prospects.

☐ Put any loose valuables in a safe place out of sight.

☐ Schedule visits 30-45 minutes apart.

☐ Log the names and phone numbers of all prospects who will give them to you. (Guest list form provided)

☐ Try to end the showing with a point of action; ideally, the arrangement of a second visit or meeting in another location to discuss the sale further.

GUEST LOG FOR YOUR OPEN HOUSES

Name	Address	Phone Number

HOW TO AMERICA, INC.

HOME SALES KIT™

CHECKLIST OF QUESTIONS TO ASK REAL ESTATE AGENTS

Agents can be invaluable in helping you price your home and speed your sale. You should never be concerned about the ethical propriety of seeking the advice of an agent who you don't plan to list your home with. This agent may, after all, have a chance to make some money on your home's sale...it just won't be as much money as usual. Also, consider your contact with agents the establishment of a long-term business relationship. If you ever do list a property with an agent, you'll be inclined to use one who was helpful to you as a self-seller.

The following are a few of the basic questions you should not hesitate to ask agents who are familiar with home sales in your area.

☐ What is the general condition of the home sales market in your area right now? How much do they feel your home is worth?

☐ How long do they think it should take to sell your house at the price they recommend?

☐ Can they recommend any good real estate lawyers?

☐ What are the best bargains for home financing right now, and which lenders are offering them?

☐ What are the best publications to advertise in? Which advertising sections and days of the week are most suitable for ad placement?

☐ Can they recommend any improvements for your home that would expedite a sale?

☐ How much, if any, of a reduction in commission rate would they be willing to accept if they provided a buyer for your home?

☐ Which real estate brokerages are most active in home sales in your area?

NOTES:

HOW TO AMERICA, INC.

Qualifying buyers

QUALIFYING BUYERS

Especially for the self-seller, selling time is precious. When a professional agent is working to sell your home, most of the time spent in the sales effort is not your own. But when you're on your own timeclock, every minute counts. After a few time-consuming but unproductive discussions with half-hearted, tire-kicking home shoppers, you will quickly become convinced of the importance of qualifying your buyers.

The telephone is your first line of defense against time wasters. You need to cast aside time-wasters by asking fair, but direct questions about their personal finances with interested prospects. Be prepared to ask them such questions as their combined family income…the quality of their credit rating…the size of total household debts…and how much cash they have available for a down payment. If otherwise interested prospects are evasive or embarrassed about disclosing such information, don't push. Their true buying power will be revealed soon enough by the lenders that they try to borrow from. But it is to your advantage to try to coax such particulars out of prospects as early as possible; because there are far too many buyers who unfortunately talk much bigger than they can buy.

In order to screen your callers, you should be familiar with the qualifying parameters that lenders typically apply. These criteria vary according to a given lender's eagerness to make a loan and a given borrower's overall quality of credit and character. For the right borrower, these rules can be bent to the breaking point, and often are–but that will be the lender's decision, not yours. The important thing is that you have at least a basic grasp of the following "rule of thumb" factors used by most lenders to qualify borrowers of residential loans.

Income. Lenders measure gross monthly income, not take-home pay, when evaluating a borrower's ability to afford a mortgage payment. It is commonly accepted that home mortgage payments should not exceed 25 to 28% of a borrower's monthly gross income. If a couple is borrowing, the income of both are combined for consideration.

Total debts. The lender will take a buyer's anticipated mortgage payment and add it to all other borrower debts, including monthly car, credit card, and all other revolving credit and real estate payments. The total amount of monthly debt payments, including home mortgage, should not exceed 35% of monthly gross pre-tax income.

Cash on hand. A lender will expect the buyer to have enough cash to cover the proposed down payment (10% of the sales price on a 90% loan, or 20% of the sales price on an 80% loan); all of the borrower's portion of closing costs (these are detailed later in the book); plus at least three months of mortgage payments left over in savings.

The amount of a mortgage payment is dictated by :
• the size of the mortgage
• the interest rate of the mortgage
• the term of the mortgage

Figuring a mortgage payment is really not hard, once you know these three pieces of information. To make it even easier, we have included loan amortization table that will let you quickly compute payments for the most common residential loan conditions.

The term, or amortization period of most home loans is 30 years. Recent years have seen an emergence of popularity for the 15-year loan, which involves a somewhat higher monthly payment and a slightly lower interest rate than its 30-year counterpart. Fans of 15-year mortgages like them because of the obvious advantage of faster equity accumulation; a home can be paid off in half the time consumed by most home loans.

Most people still prefer the traditional 30-year term and its lower payment. Many people don't realize that they can have the best of both loans by making surplus payments on a regular 30-year loan, and simply requesting that the lender apply the overpayment to the principal of the loan only. But this information is only for your background–you might confuse an unfamiliar buyer with a lot of specialized loan variations.

The best thing to do is keep it simple. Here is an example of how to figure a monthly mortgage payment, based on a hypothetical $100,000 sales price.

$100,000 Price
-10,000 10% down payment (on a 90% loan)
$90,000 Mortgage balance

Let's assume that your buyer secures a 30-year, 10% mortgage for the $90,000 balance.

HOW TO AMERICA, INC.

Find the multiplier for 10% on the 30-year mortgage payment table (8.78), and multiply that number by the number of thousands in the balance owed.

90 x 8.78 = a monthly mortgage payment of $790.20

This amount includes principal and interest (referred to as P&I). To this amount, you must add one-twelfth of the property's annual taxes and insurance costs (T&I). This total payment, including principal, interest, taxes, and insurance is often abbreviated as the PITI.

Use the enclosed tables to determine approximate P&I payments on your house for 90% (10% down) and 80% (20% down) mortgages on both the 30- and 15-year amortization periods. Then add taxes and insurance for the total PITI payment. This way you will be able to respond with specific payments to fit any prospect's preferred means of financing.

Another important qualifier for your prospects—make sure they don't plan to hang you up with any contingencies. A favorite buyer's complication is the need to sell a house of their own before they can buy your or anyone else's. Some buyers ask sellers to accept an offer subject to the sale of the buyer's house within a stipulated period. In all but the hottest real estate markets, this is a bad deal for the seller because it would allow a single prospect to hold up your house for an extended time during which you'd be precluded from selling to anyone else. If the buyer's house doesn't sell, you're out of luck and minus months of precious time.

Also beware of buyers' contingencies that demand any other special provisions besides reasonable inspections, document approval by the buyer's attorney and/or accountant, and the securing of financing within a reasonable period (this period will depend on how busy the lenders are in your area, but should not exceed 60 days in any case).

Having your lender pre-qualify

Once you're fairly confident that you have a viable prospect on your hands, it is time for you to arrange for a lender's pre-qualification of your buyer. The best way to handle this is to refer the buyer to a lender with which you or the buyer already have a relationship. If you don't already have such a relationship where you or your buyer have loan, savings, checking, or credit card accounts, simply select a reputable lender in your area and request a loan officer. Ask this contact to work up a list detailing all of the costs associated with originating a home loan based on your estimated selling price. Also ask the contact to specify other required borrower material—like tax returns, financial statements, etc.

The loan officer will be happy to provide this information, either over the phone, or on a form that you can pick up or receive by mail (WE HAVE INCLUDED A SAMPLE). This will allow you to offer authoritative input on both your home's mortgage payment, and the total expenses that a loan for your home will cost your buyer at closing.

Also ask your lender to compile similar information on the various adjustable rate mortgages (ARMs) they have available. By starting a home loan out with payments based on interest rates substantially below market rates, ARMs allow buyers to afford homes that they would be otherwise unable to qualify for. Know your ARMs—in these days of uncertain interest rates and more strict lender qualifying standards, ARMs may make all the difference between making and losing a sale.

After you have briefed your buyer on the particulars of the preferred loan approaches, arrange to have the prospect visit the lender you have been dealing with. Of course, you should not object if your buyer prefers to deal with another lender. All you care about is seeing that financing is arranged for the sale, regardless of who the lender is.

The lender can typically pre-qualify a prospect within a few days, or often hours, of interviewing the borrower and reviewing the borrower's finances. Feel free to call the lender shortly after the interview, and ask for an appraisal of the borrower's acceptability for the purchase of your home. The enclosed standard residential loan application form shows you the kinds of things a lender will want to know about its borrowers.

When that wondrous time arrives that you have what appears to be a legitimate buyer—or even more than one buyer interested in your home—force yourself to stay cool and avoid overconfidence. Even the most promising prospects can turn out to be duds. Brace yourself for possible disappointment...but maintain the justified confidence that victory will be yours.

HOW TO AMERICA, INC.

QUESTIONS TO ASK YOUR PROSPECTS

      In addition to the name, address, and phone number that you ask prospects to record on your guest log, you should fill out your own questionnaire for each prospect, that records the answers, to the below questions. If prospects are reluctant to answer any of these, don't push; but this information can be valuable and time-saving for you if you can get it. They are calling you either because they drove by and saw your sign, received a leaflet or are in response to your ad.

☐   Desired home size – Approximate square footage

☐   Desired number of bedrooms and baths

☐   Desired lot size

☐   Is a fireplace required?

☐   Do you want a formal dining room and/or family room?(these are critical points for many buyers)

☐   How soon do you plan to buy?

☐   Do you have to sell your own home before you can buy another one?

☐   Do you currently own or rent?

☐   How much money are you willing to provide for a down payment?

☐   How is your credit?

☐   Are you currently employed? Is your spouse?

☐   Are you working with any lenders? Have you been pre-qualified by a lender for a specific purchase amount and mortgage payment?

☐   Are you seeking to buy with VA or FHA financing? (These financing options enable buyers to more easily qualify for a mortgage)

☐   Where are you currently employed? How long have you worked there?

☐   Is this home in the price range that you can afford?

☐   What are the approximate gross monthly earning of you and your spouse?

☐   What is the approximate amount of your total monthly installment debt (excluding current housing costs)?

☐   Do you like our home? If so, when can we get together again?

CREDIT INFORMATION FORM

Name: _____

Social Security Number: _____

Home phone: _____

Work phone: _____

Address: _____

_____

       ☐ own   ☐ rent for $_____/mo. from_____

       Phone:_____

Previous address if less than 2 years at current address:

_____

_____

Name, address and phone of employer:

_____

_____

_____

       Title:_____

       How long with employer:_____

If less than 2 years, name, address and phone of previous employer:

_____

_____

_____

       Title:_____

       How long with employer:_____

If less than 2 years, name, address and phone of previous employer:

_____

_____

_____

       Title:_____

       How long with employer:_____

Current monthly gross income: $_____

Creditors (include holders of credit card and charge accounts):

Name	Address	Account Number

HOW TO AMERICA, INC.

HOME SALES KIT ™

Other credit references:

_____

_____

Assets:

1. Checking and savings accounts

   Bank   Address

   _____ $ _____

   _____ $ _____

   _____ $ _____

   _____ $ _____

2. Stocks and bonds

   _____ $ _____

   _____ $ _____

   _____ $ _____

   _____ $ _____

3. Real Estate

   Market value: $_____ Mortgages/lien: $_____ Net Equity: $ _____

4. Vehicles (make, year and market value)

   _____ $ _____

   _____ $ _____

5. Business

   _____ $ _____

   _____ $ _____

6. Other

   _____ $ _____

   _____ $ _____

Total assets $_____

Liabilities:		Unpaid Balance	Monthly Payment
1.	Real estate loans _____	$ _____	$ _____
2.	Spousal/child support _____	$ _____	$ _____
3.	Vehicle loans _____	$ _____	$ _____
4.	Other _____	$ _____	$ _____

Total $_____ Monthly total $_____

   We authorize_____to verify our deposits with all banks, savings and
loan associations, credit unions, and stockbrokers listed above. We further authorize

_____to receive any and all information about our credit from
credit-reporting agencies and to verify employment with the employers listed above.

_____ _____,19____

_____ _____,19____

MONTHLY PAYMENTS / Based on $12,000

Interest Rate	Length of Mortgage			
	15 years	20 years	25 years	30 years
8	$114.72	$100.44	$92.64	$88.08
8 1/4	116.52	102.36	94.68	90.24
8 1/2	118.20	104.16	96.72	92.28
8 3/4	120.00	106.08	98.76	94.44
9	121.88	108.00	100.80	96.60
9 1/4	123.60	109.92	102.84	98.76
9 1/2	125.40	111.96	104.88	100.92
9 3/4	127.20	113.88	107.04	103.20
10	128.95	115.80	109.08	105.36
10 1/4	130.79	117.84	111.12	107.52
10 1/2	132.65	119.76	113.28	109.80
10 3/4	134.51	121.80	115.44	111.96
11	136.39	123.84	117.60	114.24
11 1/4	138.28	125.88	119.76	116.52
11 1/2	140.18	127.92	121.92	118.80
11 3/4	142.10	130.80	124.20	121.08
12	144.02	132.12	126.36	123.48
12 1/4	145.96	134.23	128.61	125.75
12 1/2	147.90	136.34	130.84	128.07
12 3/4	149.86	138.46	133.90	130.40
13	151.83	140.59	135.34	132.74
13 1/4	153.81	142.73	137.60	135.09
13 1/2	155.80	144.88	139.88	137.45
13 3/4	157.80	147.05	142.16	139.81
14	159.81	149.22	144.45	142.18
14 1/4	161.82	151.41	146.75	144.56
14 1/2	163.90	153.60	149.06	146.95
14 3/4	165.90	155.80	151.38	149.34
15	167.95	158.01	153.70	151.73
15 1/4	170.01	160.24	156.03	154.14
15 1/2	172.08	162.47	158.37	156.54
15 3/4	174.16	164.70	160.71	158.95
16	176.24	166.95	163.07	161.37

Example: Loan amount @ 10% on $85,000 at 30 years. Take the 10% figure ($105.36) and divide by 12 ($12,000) and multiply it by 85 ($85,000 loan amount) $105.36 ÷ 12 ($12,000) = $8.78 (per $1,000) x 85 ($85,000 loan amount) total $746.30 approximate payment at 10% for 30 years.

NOTES:

ASK YOUR LENDER

This is an example of what a lender will do for you free of charge. Call around to see which lenders or mortgage brokers have this information. You can actually request all this by phone and have them send it, so that you can make copies. This will help you prequalify your buyers and they can see approximately what all the expenses and costs will be to them as well. Use the asking price to get your figures.

	Program 1	Program 2	Program 3
Loan Type	FHA 203B	Federal VA	Conv. Fixed
Sales Price	$74,900	$74,900	$74,900
Base Loan amt.	$72,800	$74,900	$71,100
MIP/VA Fund. Fee Financed	$2,766	$749	$0
Loan Amount	$75,566	$75,649	$71,100
Down Payment	$2,100	$0	$3,800
Interest Rate	10.000%	10.000%	10.000%
Loan Term (years)	30	30	30
Number of Units	1	1	1
Discount Points	2.5	0	2
Annual Taxes	$1,729	$1,729	$1,729

ESTIMATED MONTHLY PAYMENTS;

Principle & Interest	$663.15	$663.87	$623.95
Taxes	144.08	144.08	144.08
Fire Insurance	14.00	14.00	14.00
Mortgage Insurance	0.00	0.00	26.00
Total Monthly Payment:	$821.23	$821.96	$808.04

CLOSING COSTS -Estimated:

Loan Origination Fee 1%	$728.00	$749.00	$711.00
Mortgage Insurance	0.00	0.00	799.00
Loan Discount Points	1,889.15	0.00	1,422.00
Title Insurance	142.00	142.00	138.00
Appraisal Fee	250.00	250.00	250.00
Credit Report	48.00	48.00	48.00
Document Preparation Fee	0.00	0.00	0.00
Escrow Fee	137.00	0.00	137.00
County Transfer Tax	37.00	37.00	37.00
Recording Fees	25.00	25.00	25.00
VA Funding Fee	0.00	749.00	0.00
Buydown Points	0.00	0.00	0.00
Tax Service Fee	0.00	0.00	54.00
Estimated Closing Costs:	$3,256.15	$1,251.00	$3,621.00

PREPAID EXPENSES - Estimated:

Prepaid Interest 30 days	$621.09	$621.77	$584.38
Property Tax Reserve	$1,440.83	$1,440.83	$1,440.83
Fire Insurance Reserve	$196.00	$196.00	$196.00
Estimated Prepaid Costs	$2,257.92	$2,258.61	$2,221.22
Closing Costs & Prepaids:	$5,514.07	$3,509.61	$5,842.22
Downpayment Required:	$2,100.00	$0.00	$3,800.00
Estimated Total Needed:	$7,614.07	$3,509.61	$9,642.22

This form does not cover all possible items you may be required to pay in cash at settlement. This is only an estimate of settlement costs.

HOW TO AMERICA, INC.

MOVE IN COST ESTIMATE FORM

PURCHASER:_____

PROPERTY ADDRESS: _____

SALES PRICE ....$ _____

1st Mtge/Contract Balance ....$ _____

Down Payment ....$ _____

ESTIMATED LOAN AND CLOSING COSTS:

Loan Fee ....$ _____

Loan Discount ....$ _____

Credit Report ....$ _____

Assumption Fee ....$ _____

Appraisal Fee ....$ _____

Survey ....$ _____

Escrow Fee ....$ _____

Mortgagee's Title Ins. (ALTA) ....$ _____

Transfer Taxes ....$ _____

Recording Fees ....$ _____

Interest To Date of Closing ....$ _____

Private Mortgage Ins. Premium ....$ _____

Home Inspection Fee ....$ _____

Legal fees ....$ _____

TOTAL ESTIMATED COSTS ....$ _____

ESTIMATED RESERVES AND PRO:RATES:

Tax Reserves   Months ....$ _____

Tax Pro-Rates   Months ....$ _____

Fire Insurance Premium 12 Months ...$ _____

TOTAL ESTIMATED RESERVES AND PRO-RATES ....$ _____

TOTAL ESTIMATED CASH OUTLAY ....$ _____

ESTIMATED MONTHLY PAYMENT:

1st Mortgage: Loan Type_____Years_____Rate of Interest_____

Principle, Interest& Mtge. Ins. ....$ _____

Tax Reserves ....$ _____

Insurance Reserves ....$ _____

ESTIMATED TOTAL MONTHLY PAYMENT: ....$ _____

This transaction will be closed in escrow or by a lawyer. Final closing procedures and figures are the responsibility of the escrow agent, or your lawyer.

THESE FIGURES ARE ESTIMATES ONLY

_____   _____
Purchaser   Purchaser

All computations based for Approximate Closing Date of_____, 19_____

Your Title or Escrow Company will be able to help you with fees and taxes for this form based on actual selling price. We suggest to have the figures based on the asking price. You can receive this information by phone, in writing or through a personal visit.

HOW TO AMERICA, INC.

Writing your earnest money

WRITING YOUR EARNEST MONEY

When you've done your job and have a **qualified** buyer on your hands, it's time to find out just how serious that prospect is by moving on to the offer-writing stage as quickly as possible.

When it comes to agreement on price, you must be prepared for the age-old ritual of haggling, especially with a big-ticket item like a home. Only the most naive buyers or strongest real estate markets will produce full-price offers with regularity. Under typical circumstances, expect counter-offers that, on a sales price of $125,000 or less, may range from $5,000 to $20,000 or more off your asking price. Since you should have already prepared for this tradition by "buffering" your asking price with some maneuvering room, you will be ready to accommodate counters without compromising your true bottom line price.

You may encounter a forthright buyer who cuts right to the bone by asking you what the lowest price you are willing to accept is. Don't be afraid; this is a fair question. You should already have well established in your mind what your bottom line price is and you should be willing, under certain circumstances, to disclose it. Those circumstances are that you qualify this price as a true "lowest price" which you honestly can't go below. If this price is not low enough for your direct buyer, your sincerity will have weeded out a time-waster. If on the other hand the buyer appreciates your willingness to skip the game playing and get down to business, you may win a sale as well as the buyer's respect.

Ask for an offer

Regardless of the approaches or personalities of your buyers: if they seem to have interest, don't let them get away without gently challenging them to make an offer. This prodding may get them to open up about any objections they may have about your house, and help advance the sales process a step closer to a point of real action. This stage of greater openness should not be considered an invitation to debate, but an opportunity for you to answer any concerns a buyer may have with pleasant, positive rebuttals.

If the buyer appears to be in an undecided phase of flirting with the idea of buying your house, allow some breathing room. As always, try to get a phone number and suggest that the two of you get together in a few days to reassess...but don't wait too long.

As in any other sales task, time is of the essence. It's all too easy for would-be buyers to cool off fast unless they're steadily guided onward toward a state of demonstrated commitment. That is why the writing of an earnest money agreement is such an important milestone; for the first time, it takes the home sales process beyond the talking stages and into the sacred realm of execution.

The term "earnest money" means exactly what it says...it is a buyer's deposit of funds intended to add earnest substance to a buyer's announced intention to buy. For most residential transactions, earnest money amounts range from 1% to 1-$\frac{1}{2}$% of the home sales price, with $1,000 being a payment commonly accepted.

You will need to consult a lawyer to develop some form of earnest money agreement. **Laws vary enough from state to state to make a lawyer's review virtually mandatory for you to assure that your best interests are being protected.**

A review of the basic earnest money agreement is a routine, relatively brief, and therefore quite affordable service. The review should be **before** the agreement is signed. A earnest money agreement is a binding legal document.

The purpose of the earnest money is twofold: to demonstrate serious intent by the buyer, as previously discussed, and to legally document the details of the proposed transaction. As you'll see our earnest money agreement will specify:

- Sales price of home
- Down payment
- Resulting balance to be owed by buyer
- How and when the balance will be paid
- Date the buyer is to take possession of the property
- Specification of how closing costs are to be shared (the split is often 50-50; closing costs are often 1-2% of the sales price)
- Provision for prorating, or proportionate sharing, of taxes and other home expenses such as rent, insurance, and utilities as mutually agreed by the buyer and seller.

Other common, but not universal elements found in earnest money agreements include the

HOW TO AMERICA, INC.

seller's agreement to provide title insurance free of any undisclosed encumbrances…a seller's warranty that the property will be delivered in acceptable condition at closing…and arrangement for additional buyer's inspections of the house if desired.

Another key provision that is too often omitted from offers drawn both by professionals and self-sellers is the seller's requirement that the buyer must apply for financing within a strictly specified period of time (three working days is our recommendation). Without this stipulation, buyers have a loophole that allows them to stall the sale while using "busy schedules" or "uncooperative lenders" as excuses. Three working days is a reasonable period of time for most earnest buyers to submit a loan application to a lender.

For those buyers whose unique work or personal schedules genuinely preclude accommodation of this seller's request, allowances can be made for the sake of preserving the sale. The moral, however, is to avoid allowing any single prospect to string you along too far without furnishing evidence of steady, timely pursuit of the borrowing process. Too many sellers who failed to put limits on buyers have discovered too late that their buyers, while serious, are not financially qualified to buy. The objective in all phases of your sales process is to minimize and if possible eliminate the amount of time that you waste, or allow others to waste for you.

Another precaution: allow for some flexibility in the closing date that is provided for in your earnest money agreement. The closing of the sale of real estate is often a cumbersome process, at best. By the time you tally the cumulative delays of attorney's review of the earnest money agreement, your buyer's attorney's review of the earnest money agreement, your buyer's lender's processing of the buyer's loan, your title company's consolidation and processing of all involved documentation, and a possible second review of the modified paperwork by the attorney's for both parties, it is easy to see why there tend to be far more late home sale closings than early ones.

Yet in the midst of all these potential delays, you have the highly charged emotions of buyers who are about to make the largest and most significant purchase of their lifetime. It is the destabilizing effect of this unsettling atmosphere that can convert perfectly responsible, businesslike individuals into anxiety-wracked zombies. The dangerous culmination of all this stress is last minute, pre-closing buyer's remorse, more commonly known as cold feet. It is to your advantage to stay as calm, cool, and collected as possible.

Allow for flexibility

For all of these reasons, skittish buyers may panic if paperwork isn't completed as the agreed closing date approaches. That is why we suggest that you refer to closing dates in this manner: "Closing to occur on (date), or as soon thereafter as the preparation of necessary paperwork allows." This simple latitude can do a lot to reassure nail-biting buyers and you the seller, as the finish line approaches. Thanks to this simple statement, all parties can be assured that missing a preset closing date does not necessarily spell doom for the deal.

If the buyers are knowledgeable, they may require the earnest money agreement make reference to your responsibility for repairs as required either as a result of inspections by the buyer and/or an inspector, or lender's appraiser. It is common for the seller to absorb such costs, but you should also insist that this requirement be qualified with a repair budget limit in order to protect yourself. If your buyer insists on addressing the repair issue in the earnest money agreement, be sure to temper it with a statement such as "seller agrees to pay for specific repairs as enumerated herein. If additional repairs are deemed necessary by a lender in order to close the transaction, seller agrees to pay not more than $ ___, including materials and labor for said repairs."

Then, all repairs required by your buyer and agreed to by you should be listed in an attachment, or "addendum," to your earnest money agreement. By setting a limit on the dollars you're willing to spend on home repairs, your are protecting yourself from responsibility for an extravagant "wish list" of home improvements that some appraiser, inspector, or "expert" buyer's friends might unexpectedly concoct.

In order to expedite your sale, you should attach reasonable time limits to every contingency. As already mentioned, the buyer should be required to make immediate application to a lender. The buyer should also be

HOW TO AMERICA, INC.

confined to a 4 to 7 day period during which all buyer's inspections should occur, whether they are to be made by a bona fide inspector or curious Aunt Minnie.

It is the buyer's job to set these inspections up in accordance with your schedule, which you should of course make as accommodating as possible. Also, the cost of any professional inspection should be covered by the buyer. On the other hand, the cost of a property survey–to verify the legal location of property lines–is normally the seller's expense. However, it is rarely asked for by most buyers (many don't).

Keep things moving

As seller, your goal is to keep things moving as quickly as possible. You must resolve to be part pest and part cheerleader as you diplomatically prod and push all parties to the sale along. As mentioned before, you should call the buyer's lender right after the buyer has applied. That contact will be just the beginning. You must continue to stay in touch with the lender's loan officer who has been assigned to your buyer's loan at least every few days. Contrary to the cliches, most "holdups" at financial institutions are not committed by ski-masked desperados brandishing pistols, but rather by the staff in the loan department; and customers like your buyer and you are the victims.

Lenders are notorious for letting loan applications, or "loan aps" sit unnoticed in a stack until somebody complains loudly enough to get it moved a little closer to the top of the pile. This is a classic example of the squeaky wheel getting the grease. In all too many cases, you must be a polite but persistent nag for your buyer with his lender. This is a role the conscientious real estate agent would normally perform, and one that you can't expect the buyer to understand. As a self-seller, this becomes one of your simple, but necessary housekeeping tasks.

We earlier touched on the warning to avoid allowing the sale of your house to be contingent on the sale of your buyer's home. The acceptance by you of this arrangement should remain a truly last-ditch option for you. Only if you're stuck in a terrible real estate market, and if you are particularly confident of the interest level and substance of your buyer, and if your buyer has already pre-qualified with a

lender…only then might you consider this frankly undesirable sales technique.

If you do consider your sale contingent on your buyer's sale, however, **be sure to protect yourself with a "72-hour contingency."** Under this arrangement, you may continue to market your home while awaiting your buyer's sale of his house to perform on his offer for yours. If you develop another buyer for your home, at any time, you are merely required to notify your first buyer, preferably by certified mail with return receipt requested, that he now has 72 hours in which to confirm his purchase of your house in accordance with the terms specified in your earnest money agreement. If he is unable to respond within the 72 hours, he forfeits his claim on your house, and you are free to complete your sale to your second buyer. You must, however, return the first buyer's earnest money.

Our recommendation is that if you ever accept an offer on you home subject to a buyer's sale, you continue to market your house as aggressively as you would if you had no sale at all–because there is a real possibility that your contingent sale may not work out, particularly within your time frame.

For title or escrow

Once you have all the elements completed in your earnest money agreement; home sales price, terms of sale, tentative closing date, contingencies, sharing of closing costs, and prorating of other costs through closing, you are ready to open your escrow account. If your buyer is unfamiliar with this aspect of a real estate transaction, explain that an escrow company is a neutral third party that holds a buyer's earnest money until closing, and assists in the preparation of all paperwork necessary to complete your sale/the buyer purchase of your home.

The escrow company is an independent hired agent who lends professional integrity and objectivity to the process, and assures your buyer that he will get good and sufficient title and proper documentation of his home purchase. **The buyers check or note for earnest money should be made out in the name of the escrow company that you and your buyer have agreed upon (a check is preferable**–it will be immediately cashed and held by the escrow company). Once again, have your attorney review your earnest money agreement before it

HOW TO AMERICA, INC.

is signed or submitted to escrow.

From this point forward the escrow company will be the central point of coordination for the processing and recording of all documents to complete your sale. Like lenders, escrow companies can be stall points for home sales, especially in active real estate markets. You must be as diligent and regular in your contact with your escrow company as you are with your buyer's lender.

Arranging a closing date

Another key issue—and one that can be a source of great headache as closing time approaches, is the distinction between the "possession date" and "closing date" of your home sale. Your earnest money agreement may stipulate that closing is expected to occur by, say

January 1, 19__ , and that your buyer may take possession of the premises within five days after closing. The buyer and seller then proceed to base all of their respective transition plans on a closing date whose questionable reliability we have already discussed. What if closing is late, as it so often is? Yet the buyer's current dwelling has already been rented or sold, and you, too, are expected to occupy your new residence, based on the January 1 closing date.

To avoid the grief that usually accompanies this possibility you should prepare for the worst at the start—in your earnest money agreement. You must decide at the beginning which party – buyer or seller – most urgently needs to be in your house, when closing time arrives. As the seller, you are probably inclined to be more lenient in order to make the sale, but of course that's your decision.

NOTES:

HOW TO AMERICA, INC.

HOW TO HIRE THE RIGHT LAWYER

Make sure your lawyer is experienced in residential real estate law.

Make clear to your lawyer the responsibilities expected; that you expect to be advised of all services that the lawyer feels should be offered you in order to assure an orderly and safe transaction.

If you sell on a contract, your lawyer should be experienced in drawing such documents.

The lawyer should complete the earnest money agreement or review it before you sign it.

All buyer or/and seller contingencies should be reviewed by your lawyer before the earnest money is signed.

The lawyer should have an opportunity to review all closing documents before they are signed by either buyer or seller.

Have the lawyer pay special attention to your sales agreement's references to the closing and possession dates. Make sure any provisions for buyer occupancy of your house before closing are thoroughly reviewed and approved by your lawyer.

Checklist for hiring a lawyer

☐ Ask your family lawyer for a recommendation, if he or she does not do real estate.

☐ Are your lawyer's fees going to be reasonable? Pose this question before services are engaged, not after.

☐ Ask what circumstances would warrant an increase in the fee estimate your lawyer gives you.

☐ How will document review take place – at your lawyer's office or elsewhere?(This could have a significant impact on your cost.)

☐ Is your lawyer of choice fairly active in residential home law? Ask. If you have any doubts, check with your local state bar association.

☐ Make sure your lawyer can be reached outside of normal business hours – just in case.

☐ Ask if billings will be itemized, so you can track which aspects of legal assistance were the most costly (this is good for future reference).

☐ Just so you know, ask how much will it cost to prepare a land sales contract.

☐ Make sure you have a lawyer **before** writing your Earnest Money.

"HOME SALES KIT"™
TERMS OF SALE SHEET

1. Seller's Name, Address and Telephone Number:

   _____

   _____

   _____

2. Buyer's Name, Address and Telephone Number:

   _____

   _____

   _____

3. Property Address:

   _____

   _____

   _____

4. Purchase Price:_____

   A. Earnest Money: _____

   B. Downpayment at Closing:_____

   C. Payment Terms on Balance: _____

5. Proposed Closing Date:_____

6. Personal Property Included in Sale:

   _____

   _____

   _____

7. Additional Contingencies (i.e., financing, inspections, etc.):

   _____

   _____

   _____

   _____

**THIS DOCUMENT IS SOLELY FOR THE CONVENIENCE OF THE PARTIES.
THIS IS NOT A BINDING AGREEMENT**

This form is to be used if not using the Earnest Money we have enclosed. Your lawyer will be able to write a legal contract from this form.

HOW TO AMERICA, INC.

"HOME SALES KIT"™
TERMS OF SALE SHEET

1. Seller's Name, Address and Telephone Number:

   _____

   _____

   _____

2. Buyer's Name, Address and Telephone Number:

   _____

   _____

   _____

3. Property Address:

   _____

   _____

   _____

4. Purchase Price:_____

   A. Earnest Money: _____

   B. Downpayment at Closing:_____

   C. Payment Terms on Balance: _____

5. Proposed Closing Date:_____

6. Personal Property Included in Sale:

   _____

   _____

   _____

7. Additional Contingencies (i.e., financing, inspections, etc.):

   _____

   _____

   _____

   _____

THIS DOCUMENT IS SOLELY FOR THE CONVENIENCE OF THE PARTIES.
THIS IS NOT A BINDING AGREEMENT

This form is to be used if not using the Earnest Money we have enclosed. Your lawyer will be able to write a legal contract from this form.

INSTRUCTIONS TO ESCROW

HOME SALES KIT™

Escrow Company_____

Escrow Branch_____ Date_____

Escrow Officer_____

Property _____
        (Address)   (City/State)   (Zip)

_____
                          (Legal Description)

Seller_____
                          (Names)

_____
        (Address)   (City/State)   (Zip)

Phones_____ Attorney_____
    (Home)   (Office)

Buyer_____
                         (Names)

_____
        (Address)   (City/State)   (Zip)

Phones_____ Attorney_____
    (Home)   (Office)

Sales Price $_____ Terms_____

Existing Loan with_____ Loan No. _____

New Loan with_____ Loan Officer_____
        (Company/Branch)

NOTE: The information thay you have provided above should accompany the Earnest Money check and a copy of the Sales Agreement to your attorney or escrow officer

HOW TO AMERICA, INC.

CHECKLIST TO INSURE EASIER CLOSING

INSTRUCTIONS:

Title Co. _____

Escrow Officer _____

Phone Number_____

Date Opened Escrow_____

Check with Escrow Officer weekly to make sure all is well & moving along

Date Checked with Escrow _____ _____ _____ _____ _____

Your Purchaser's Lender _____

Loan officer_____

Phone Number_____

Loan application date_____

Appraisal date_____ Time_____

Appraiser's name _____

Check with Loan Officer weekly for credit approval, appraisal approval, loan approval.

Date Checked _____ _____ _____ _____ _____ _____

Home Inspector _____ (purchaser to get inspector of their choice)

Phone Number_____

Date_____ Time_____

Real estate agent (should you need)_____

phone_____wk_____hm

Your Lawyer_____ phone_____wk_____hm

Check with your Lawyer weekly_____ _____ _____ _____

Buyers Lawyer_____ phone_____wk_____hm

Close Date_____

Recording Date_____

SOME OF THE MOST COMMON HOME SALES CONTINGENCIES

☐ **Home inspection.** Home must be in reasonable condition at the point when the buyer takes occupancy. This is a standard, and reasonable provision.

☐ **Subject to sale of buyer's present home.** This is one to watch out for; it can needlessly tie up your home and works primarily to the advantage of the buyer.

☐ **Subject to buyer's qualification for financing within a certain period of time.** This is a mandatory provision to add for the seller's protection.

☐ **Subject to sale by land sales contract.** Some buyers who cannot qualify for conventional financing will make this a prerequisite of their purchase.

☐ **Subject to specific financing terms.** This is used for the buyer's benefit; a contingency of sale dependant on the buyer's securing of a mortgage payment, down payment, or interest rate not to exceed a certain amount.

☐ **Appraisal.** Another buyer's defense, to make sure that the selling price is not too high above the home's true reasonable market value.

☐ **72-hour contingency.** This is good protection for a seller, yet is fair to the buyer who wants to buy but can't due to delays (such as the sale of the buyer's current home). This guarantees the buyer of a certain sales price, but provides that if the seller finds an alternate buyer at any time, the first buyer must act on the purchase within 72 hours or lose any claim to your house.

THE FOR SALE BY OWNER KIT™
COMMON CONTINGENCIES TO EARNEST MONEY AGREEMENTS

1. Purchaser's obligation to purchase the property is subject to the Purchaser and the property qualifying for a conventional loan in the amount of $_____ at an interest rate not to exceed _____ percent. Purchaser agrees to make written application for such a loan not later than _____, 19____.
2. Purchaser shall have until _____, 19____ to inspect the condition of the property and to review such other matters pertaining to the property as Purchaser deems appropriate. If Purchaser is not satisfied with the results of the inspections, investigations and reviews, Purchaser may cancel this agreement by written notice to Seller and Purchaser's earnest money will be fully refunded to Purchaser.
3. Purchaser's obligation to purchase the property here under is subject to Purchaser selling his/her existing home at _____ at a price and upon terms satisfactory to Purchaser, and such sale closing on or before _____, 19____.

- -

NOTES:

HOW TO AMERICA, INC.

HOME SALES KIT™

72 HOUR CONTINGENCY AGREEMENT

DATE_____

THIS AGREEMENT is hereby made a part and condition of the following earnest money agreement as set forth.

Date of purchase agreement_____

Purchaser_____

Seller_____

Property Address _____

IT IS HEREBY AGREED THAT:

1. Purchasers obligation to purchase the property is contingent upon the sale and closing of purchasers' property which is located _____City of _____, County of_____, State of_____

2. Seller shall have the right to continue to advertise market the Property during the life of this agreement.

3. In the event that Seller receives another offer acceptable to Seller, on the property prior to the time of the removal of this contingency, THEN the Seller shall notify the purchaser herein of his intent to accept said subsequent offer and the purchasers shall have a period of time not to exceed 72 hours from the time of receipt of such notification in which to remove by written notice the contingency as set forth in item number one above.

4. If the Purchaser fails to remove the contingency during said 72 hour period THEN the earnest money agreement on the Sellers' property shall become null and void and of no further consequence to the parties hereto, and Seller shall return Purchasers earnest money deposit.

5. The Purchaser may at his option remove said contingency at any time prior to this agreement becoming null and void, regardless of whether Purchasers property is sold, however, written notice must be given to Seller removing the contingency.

6. This agreement shall become null and void and of no further consequence to the parties hereto on_____at 12:00 noon UNLESS the contingency shall have been removed prior thereto.

Seller_____   Purchaser_____

Seller_____   Purchaser_____

NOTE: Make copy for purchaser, lawyer and escrow.

HOW TO AMERICA, INC.

HOME SALES KIT

72 HOUR NOTIFICATION OF AN OFFER

TO:_____Purchaser(s)

In accordance with terms and conditions as set forth in "72 HOUR CONTINGENCY AGREEMENT" which is a part and condition of the earnest money agreement as set forth.

Date of Earnest Money Receipt and Contract _____

Purchaser_____

Seller_____

Property Address _____

Seller hereby notifies purchaser that another acceptable written earnest money offer to purchase has been presented to the Seller and accepted by them, subject to the above referenced transaction not being consummated.

According to the referenced addendum the purchaser now has(72) hours to deliver to the Seller a written waiver of contingency of sale of purchasers home.

Seller_____ Purchaser_____

Seller_____ Purchaser_____

Date_____Time_____ Date_____Time_____

Delivered to Purchaser by:

□ Certified Mail –return receipt requested.

□ Personal delivery by_____
      (Party delivering, sign here.)

_____
To Whom Delivered

_____
Signature of Recipient

_____
Signature of Recipient

NOTE: Make copy for purchaser, lawyer and escrow.

FHA and VHA mortgages

FHA AND VA MORTGAGES

Government-backed mortgages often suffer from a sullied reputation, but their commonality makes a basic understanding of them important for buyers and sellers alike. For both buyers and sellers, FHA and VA loans can be a great, if often frustrating financing option.

The Veterans Administration (VA) offers a variety of benefits to veterans of wartime and peacetime military service going back as far as World War II. FHA loans originated in 1934, when the Federal Housing Administration (FHA) was created to help make the American dream of home ownership a reality for a broader range of Americans.

The FHA and VA facilitate home loans not by making loans directly, but by insuring loans made by commercial lenders. In exchange for asking private lenders to offer home loans with more favorable terms than they normally would, the government guarantees that the lenders will be reimbursed if FHA and VA borrowers default.

In practical terms, this special arrangement allows FHA and VA borrowers to enjoy low or no down payments, lower interest rates, and in many cases more lenient qualifying standards for their home loans.

The prevalence of these loans attests to their popularity. Today FHA-backed loans comprise about 25% of the home loan market, and 12 million VA loans have been written since 1942. Unfortunately, many veterans are still not aware of or motivated by the outstanding value that VA loans represent; some 20 million eligible vets have never taken advantage of their unique borrowing privileges. Sadder still are the many widows of veterans who don't realize that they are entitled to the VA loan rights of their deceased husbands.

Part of the reluctance to deal with FHA and VA loans revolves around their notoriety as a pain to process. Many real estate agents are loath to deal with government-backed loans because of their renowned inconvenience relative to other home loan alternatives. But in most cases, borrowers find that thirty years of better-than-market borrowing is well worth the potential of a few weeks of extra loan processing effort.

Although these loans are federally regulated, the terms of FHA and VA loans vary from lender to lender. You would be well advised to find a lender in your area that specializes in loans of this kind to expedite their processing. Your local VA office can provide a list of VA lenders in your area.

In general, the VA allows a qualifying veteran to borrow up to $144,000 with no down payment, and at a below-market interest rate. If you are fortunate enough to be selling a home with an existing VA loan, you may enjoy the distinct marketing advantage of offering an assumable loan with an interest rate that is very possibly below the prevailing rates in your market.

This is the kind of loan that many buyers are looking for. If you have an assumable, low-interest FHA or VA loan, you should billboard that fact prominently in the ads and   flyers used to promote your home. Unlike the sellers and their agents who often associate these loans with extra hassles, many astute buyers scour their markets for such deals because they appreciate the bargain financing that often comes with them.

These buyers especially appreciate the FHA or VA "blind assumption" which enables a buyer to take over a seller's loan without the cost, complication, or delay of qualifying the seller with a lender. A blind assumption is quickly and easily accomplished with the buyer's payment of a nominal assumption fee.

If you have a government-backed loan that is blindly assumable, you may be able to command a higher price for your home because you are offering the seller immediate, low-interest financing, plus saving him a large loan fee. Remember, though, that while allowing a blind assumption of your loan is likely to sell your home faster and perhaps extract a higher selling price, it will also prolong your liability for the loan your buyer assumes. A blind assumption leaves you on the hook for the loan as the borrower of record; if your buyer defaults, the lender will look to you for continued debt service.

If you choose to allow a blind assumption of your loan, take the time to be especially cautious when qualifying your buyer's income, debts, and credit history. Just like a commercial lender, make sure you have a full credit report run by your local credit bureau. Call the

accounting department of your buyer's employer to verify his employment and reported salary. Don't be too timid to ask your buyer for two years of tax returns, plus receipts to confirm his reported assets of stock, savings accounts, etc.

You are doing any buyer a favor by allowing a blind assumption of your loan. If a buyer takes offense at your "nosiness," it may be a tipoff that the buyer has something to hide. Checking your buyer's creditworthiness thoroughly is a good, prudent business practice whether you are selling your home on contract or allowing a blind assumption of a government-backed loan.

As a final precaution when selling with a blind assumption, you may want to insist that your buyer make payments on the assumed loan through an escrow service. In this arrangement, the seller sends monthly payments to the service, which then notifies the seller that the buyer either has or hasn't made his loan payment in a timely manner.

This setup readily alerts the seller to any interruption of a buyer's payments on the loan, and should let you sleep a little better at night knowing that your buyer can't get more than a month behind on his mortgage payments without your knowledge. The service costs very little and can be paid for by either buyer or seller.

Because FHA and VA loans carry below-market interest rates, the lenders that offer them must compensate themselves for the difference between the artificially low rates and the true market rates prevailing in the marketplace. This compensation takes the form of "discount points" the seller pays to the lender when the loan is closed.

Each point is 1% of the amount being borrowed. Points can fluctuate rapidly, and can suddenly escalate to high levels with little or no warning. The volatility of points to be paid on government-backed loans is particularly critical for you, the seller, since points are usually paid by the seller.

Points can, therefore, significantly alter your anticipated proceeds from a sale virtually overnight. If your buyer plans to buy your home using FHA or VA financing, get educated early on about the latest status of points in your market and the lender forecasts of how high point levels may be headed.

Probably the most appealing feature of VA loans is that veterans can obtain them with no down payment. The VA requires no down payment if a home's purchase price does not exceed its value as determined by a VA appraisal. If the sales price is higher than the appraised value, the buyer must make up the difference.

FHA loans don't eliminate down payments like VA loans can, but they do provide for down payments as low as about 3% of the home's purchase price, depending on which FHA program is used. Your buyer's lender will match the buyer with the FHA program most appropriate for the purchase of your home.

Because low-down loans pose a higher degree of risk to the lender, FHA loans involving less than 20% down require a mortgage insurance premium, paid by the buyer, that amounts to 3.8% of the amount borrowed. The insurance premium is added to the loan cost in the form of a small monthly payment increase that allows the insurance premium to be paid off during the first few years of the loan.

Most buyers find this nominal mortgage insurance payment a worthwhile tradeoff for the opportunity to finance a house for as little as 3% down on an FHA loan.

Other closing costs include the VA appraisal, credit report, survey, title report, recording fees, a 1% loan origination fee, and a VA funding fee. Closing costs may not be added to the loan balance, except in the case of a VA refinance. The VA funding fee can be waived for certain buyers, such as veterans receiving compensation for service-related disabilities and surviving spouses of veterans who died in service or from a service-related disability. We mention these particulars because, again, you may have to educate qualified VA buyers about the advantages they are entitled to but unaware of.

As a seller, you should be aware of "buydowns" as another negotiating tool that pertains to FHA and VA loans. A buydown is an up-front fee paid to the lender that lowers the interest rate to be paid on the buyer's loan. A buydown can be purchased for the first few years of the loan, or for the life of the loan, depending on the size of the buydown fee paid to the lender.

Motivated sellers sometimes offer to "buy down" a buyer's interest rate to prompt a faster sale. Your local lenders can give you a rundown

on their latest menus of buydown options and costs.

For the seller, the best part about having an FHA or VA loan is that if you have such a loan existing on your home, you have a built-in marketing advantage over the competition. The drawback of these loans is that they often take more time and trouble to process and close than other loans do. Be prepared to wait four to six weeks for a loan commitment. Once you get your commitment, be further prepared for a laundry list of often nitpicky items that FHA and VA appraisers require the seller to repair.

The delays, bureaucracy, and complications of these government-backed loans can be aggravating, but if you are patient, they will eventually run their course and result in a successful closing as they have for millions of American homeowners through the years.

To the seller, the biggest advantage of FHA and VA loans is that they increase the number of buyers who can qualify to buy your home, especially if you have an assumable FHA or VA loan. One of the biggest disadvantages to the seller is that buyers may become frustrated or panicked by the chronic delays that can plague these loans. You must be prepared to reassure your buyer that obstacles are to be expected with these loans, and that those obstacles must be methodically dealt with one by one until they are all gone.

In that sense, any home loan process is like a garden that must be watered, fertilized, and fenced to protect against pests. Even with all that care, weeds will stubbornly sprout and taunt you until you pull them out, one by one.

Then you must wait...and wait some more...and pull still more weeds. But finally, like the rewards of harvest time in the garden, the rewards of closing will arrive, and you will find that the results were worth the effort.

VA REGIONAL OFFICE ADDRESS LIST

If you work with a VA buyer who wants more information about his benefits, look for the nearest VA office in your local phone book. As a backup, here is a list of regional VA offices that you can direct your VA buyers to for complete information about their loan entitlements and other benefits.

ALABAMA
VA Regional Office
474 South Court Street
Montgomery, AL 36104

ALASKA
VA Regional Office
235 East 8th Avenue
Anchorage, AK 99501

ARIZONA
VA Regional Office
3225 North Central Avenue
Phoenix, AZ 85012

ARKANSAS
VA Regional Office
1200 West 3rd Street
Little Rock, AR 72201

CALIFORNIA
VA Regional Office
Federal Building
11000 Wilshire Blvd.
Los Angeles, CA 90024

VA Regional Office
211 Main Street
San Francisco, CA 94105

COLORADO
VA Regional Office
Box 25126
44 Union Blvd.
Denver, CO 80225

CONNECTICUT
VA Regional Office
450 Main St.
Hartford, CT 06103

DELAWARE
VA Medical and Regional Office
1601 Kirkwood Highway
Wilmington, DE 19805

DISTRICT OF COLUMBIA
VA Regional Office
941 North Capitol St., NE
Washington, D.C. 20421

FLORIDA
VA Regional Office
P.O. Box 1437
144 First Avenue, South
St. Petersburg, FL 33731

GEORGIA
VA Regional Office
730 Peachtree St., NE
Atlanta, GA 30365

HAWAII
VA Regional Office
P.O. Box 50188, 96850
PJKK Federal Building
300 Ala Moana Blvd.
Honolulu, HI 96850

IDAHO
VA Regional Office
Federal Building/Courthouse
550 West Fort St.
Box 044
Boise, ID 83724

ILLINOIS
VA Regional Office
536 S. Clark St.
P.O. Box 8136
Chicago, IL 60680

INDIANA
VA Regional Office
575 North Pennsylvania St.
Indianapolis, IN 46204

IOWA
VA Regional Office
210 Walnut St.
Des Moines, IA 50309

KANSAS
VA Medical/Regional Office
901 George Washington Blvd.
Wichita, KS 67211

KENTUCKY
VA Regional Office
600 Federal Place
Louisville, KY 40202

LOUISIANA
VA Regional Office
701 Loyola Avenue
New Orleans, LA 70113

MAINE
VA Medical/Regional Office
Togus, ME 04330

MARYLAND
VA Regional Office
Federal Building
31 Hopkins Plaza
Baltimore, MD 21201

MASSACHUSETTS
VA Regional Office
John F. Kennedy Building
Government Center
Boston, MA 02203

MICHIGAN
VA Regional Office
Federal Building
477 Michigan Avenue
Detroit, MI 48226

MINNESOTA
VA Regional Office and
   Insurance Center
Federal Building
Fort Snelling
St. Paul, MN 55111

MISSISSIPPI
VA Regional Office
100 W. Capitol St.
Jackson, MS 39269

MISSOURI
VA Regional Office
Federal Building, Room 4705
1520 Market St.
St. Louis, MO 63103

MONTANA
VA Medical/Regional Office
Fort Harrison, MT 59636

NEBRASKA
VA Regional Office
Federal Building
100 Centennial Mall North
Lincoln, NE 68508

NEVADA
VA Regional Office
245 East Liberty St.
Reno, NV 89520

NEW HAMPSHIRE
VA Regional Office
Norris Cotton Federal Building
275 Chestnut St.
Manchester, NH 03101

NEW JERSEY
VA Regional Office
20 Washington Place
Newark, NJ 07102

NEW MEXICO
VA Regional Office
Federal Building/Courthouse
500 Gold Avenue, SW
Albuquerque, NM 87102

NEW YORK
VA Regional Office
Federal Building
111 West Huron St.
Buffalo, NY 14202

VA Regional Office
252 7th Ave. at 24th St.
New York, NY 10001

NORTH CAROLINA
VA Regional Office
Federal Building
251 North Main St.
Winston-Salem, NC 27155

NORTH DAKOTA
VA Medical/Regional Office
655 First Avenue North
Fargo, ND 58102

OHIO
VA Regional Office
Anthony Celebrezze Bldg.
1240 East Ninth St.
Cleveland, OH 44199

OKLAHOMA
VA Regional Office
125 S. Main St.
Muskogee, OK 74401

OREGON
VA Regional Office
Federal Building
1220 S.W. 3rd Avenue
Portland, OR 97204

PENNSYLVANIA
VA Regional Office
  and Insurance Center
P.O. Box 8079
5000 Wissahickon Avenue
Philadephia, PA 19101

VA Regional Office
1000 Liberty Avenue
Pittsburgh, PA 15222

PUERTO RICO
VA Medical/Regional Office
GPO Box 4867
San Juan, PR 00936

RHODE ISLAND
VA Regional Office
380 Westminster Mall
Providence, RI 02903

SOUTH CAROLINA
VA Regional Office
1801 Assembly St.
Columbia, SC 29201

SOUTH DAKOTA
VA Medical/Regional Office
P.O. Box 5046
2501 West 22nd St.
Sioux Falls, SD 57117

TENNESSEE
VA Regional Office
110 Ninth Avenue, South
Nashville, TN 37203

TEXAS
VA Regional Office
2515 Murworth Drive
Houston, TX 77054

VA Regional Office
1400 North Valley Mills Dr.
Waco, TX 76799

UTAH
VA Regional Office
P.O. Box 11500
125 South State St.
Salt Lake City, UT 84147

VERMONT
VA Medical/Regional Office
White River Junction, VT 05001

VIRGINIA
VA Regional Office
210 Franklin Road, SW
Roanoke, VA 24011

WASHINGTON
VA Regional Office
915 Second Avenue
Seattle, WA 98174

WEST VIRGINIA
VA Regional Office
640 4th Avenue
Huntington, WV 25701

WISCONSIN
VA Regional Office
P.O. Box 6
Milwaukee, WI 53295

WYOMING
VA Medical/Regional Office
2360 East Pershing Blvd.
Cheyenne, WY 82001

HOW TO AMERICA, INC.

Environmental considerations

ENVIRONMENTAL CONSIDERATIONS

In a handful of years, several environmental issues have emerged as potential complications within the residential real estate market. These include radon gas in the indoor air we breathe, lead-based paints in older homes, asbestos construction materials, and lead-contaminated water pipes.

These are certainly not the only environmental problems that we will have to grapple with in the coming years, but each of these issues has received a good deal of coverage and fostered a good deal of alarm.

When the radon scare first hit, radon test kits of questionable reliability sprung up on supermarket shelves. Newspapers across the country published diagrams labeled with dozens of locations where the dreaded asbestos fiber may lurk in the average American home. And fears of lead-laced water supplies have helped spawn a jump in the sale of home water purification systems.

Some of the environmental concerns facing today's homeowners are so new that their dangerousness hasn't even been defined or quantified yet. Regulatory agencies haven't yet precisely pinpointed who is most vulnerable to the adverse effects of asbestos, or how much of it can cause damage. Radon, too, poses an imprecise threat- and many municipalities around the country have no formal programs to assess and prevent lead contamination of drinking water.

Even though many of the safety standards related to these concerns are still in the developmental stages, you as a home seller should at least be aware of them; not only to protect the health of yourself and your buyer, but also to protect the health of your personal liability.

In recent years, home sellers and the real estate agents representing them have been successfully sued for attempting to cover up unsafe or undesirable characteristics of homes they've sold. Some of these "cover ups" may have been nothing more than innocent omissions by sellers, but if an intent to deceive can be established in court, a seller can be put in a legally precarious position, even long after a sale.

As in most things, honesty is the best policy when it comes to selling your home. If you are aware of defects in your home, especially those serious enough to constitute a hazard to the health and safety of future occupants, it's best to bite the bullet and disclose the problem to your buyer.

If your disclosure threatens to botch the sale, try to work out a compromise in which you and your buyer share the costs of remedying the problem. It's better to take this responsible approach early than risk a costly legal battle later.

The following is a brief review of some of the most prominent environmental issues pertaining to the residential real estate world.

Asbestos

This is one of those unfortunate materials whose versatility carried it into countless products before it was discovered to be harmful. Asbestos is a mineral that shares physical characteristics with mica, a soft rock that splits into tiny splinters at the flick of a finger. Asbestos is composed of tiny fibers, too- fibers that can cause respiratory diseases and cancer.

One of the scariest things about asbestos is that the experts don't know how much is harmful. Another scary thing is that the material seems to be hiding everywhere. It was an integral part of innumerable homes built during and prior to the 1970's in appliances, roofing, insulation, putty, gloves, gaskets, and even kitty litter. It is estimated that 80% of American homes built before 1979 contain some form of asbestos.

The ubiquity of asbestos makes its wholesale removal from the American scene impossible—there is simply too much of it in too many places. Manufacturers have, of course, eliminated asbestos from many of their products. But what about the asbestos that's already there? What should you as a homeowner and home seller do about it?

The experts say that removing asbestos can be more dangerous than leaving it where it is. If it is left undisturbed in a stable state, asbestos often doesn't pose enough danger to warrant its removal. But if you are remodeling your home in ways that cut into asbestos-bearing walls or ceilings, or if you accidentally tear water heater insulation containing asbestos, you should call a professional contractor with asbestos experience to confirm its presence and suggest a remedy.

One way to be absolutely certain that asbestos is present is through the laboratory testing of suspected material, which typically costs $20 to $40.

One of the reasons that asbestos is often not removed is that the cost of removal can be exorbitant. That's because asbestos removal contractors are burdened with heavy insurance premiums, and because some contractors insist on having air monitoring specialists present throughout a removal project to make sure contamination levels are kept to a minimum.

Examples of costs for asbestos removal in a major market in the Northwest U.S. are more than $3,000 to remove asbestos-containing "popcorn" ceiling material in a 200-square-foot room...and $2,000 to remove asbestos insulation tape from old furnace ducts.

Contractors specializing in asbestos removal conform to a strict safety protocol involving the isolation of work areas; the use of special respirators and protective clothing; the constant dampening of asbestos-bearing material to minimize airborne particles; and landfill disposal in accordance with special Environmental Protection Agency regulations. When possible, contractors will try to work around asbestos rather than risk removing it, such as installing a drop ceiling to shield an original ceiling containing asbestos above it.

Asbestos is bound to continue as an issue of concern, especially if lenders reach the point of making their financing of homes contingent on the stability or removal of asbestos in the home to be financed.

In the meantime, the initial panic about asbestos has been replaced with the pragmatic recognition that we must learn to live with the stuff. If you are worried about asbestos in your home for sale, call an experienced contractor for an evaluation. If asbestos is present, the safest course would be to advise your buyer of the fact, along with an explanation of how you have remedied or plan to remedy any asbestos-related problem to assure the buyer's safety.

Radon

Like asbestos, radon is a mysterious nuisance whose true extent of threat remains largely unknown. Radon is a natural gas that percolates up through the soil to the earth's surface. The rate of its rise can be influenced by fluctuations in the local water table. Radon is found widely throughout the U.S., although it is much more common in some areas than in others.

As radon reaches the surface of the earth, it breaks into the air and drifts away. When it breaks the surface below a house, however, it can penetrate through floors, pipe openings, and ducts beneath the house to collect in the air inside.

Radon's potential to contaminate indoor air is compounded by today's energy-efficient home construction techniques that minimize the penetration of outside air into the home. That lack of ventilation allows radon levels to build within the home.

As with asbestos, if you are concerned about radon in your home, you should have it checked by a professional. In certain regions where the problem is more common, radon is referenced in home sales agreements. Sellers may be required to make an allowance in price for professional radon testing and treatment if necessary. If the cost of treatment turns out to be considerable, a sharing of the expense can be negotiated between the buyer and seller.

If you the seller are responsible for treating a radon problem in your home, make sure that you involve a contractor experienced in radon treatment. Sometimes this is easier said than done. A friend of ours found a house he liked in Pittsburgh, so he made an offer on it subject to the seller paying for a qualified radon test.

Sure enough, the house tested positive, so the buyer got estimates to deal with the problem and persuaded the seller to reduce the sales price by the amount of the radon treatment expense. Everything was going fine until the radon "specialists" showed up in a battered van wearing respirators and dingy overalls in a scene reminiscent of the movie "Ghostbusters."

Their prescription was an elaborate system of pipes drilled into the foundation of the house to ventilate the gas, which would be driven out of the basement by a common house fan to run 24 hours a day into perpetuity. Thinking this solution a bit odd, the seller called for a second opinion from a contractor who laughed out loud when he learned that the "Radon Busters" had struck again.

The second contractor traced the radon leak to an exposed patch of dirt in the basement

HOW TO AMERICA, INC.

which he promptly poured concrete over to solve the problem. The moral—if you have a radon problem, select a radon expert that has more to offer than black magic; insist on references. Often radon problems are dealt with through enhanced ventilation, but you need to make sure it is designed properly for your specific circumstance.

Once you have a contractor that you have confidence in, the good news is that there are reliable solutions to many cases of radon contamination.

Lead paint

In former eras of environmental innocence, lead was a welcome and common ingredient in our lives. It was freely added to gasoline to optimize engine performance, and lead-based paints were considered the best. In fact, it is the durability of leaded paint that has added to its danger today.

The biggest concern about lead-based paint relates to children, particularly infants. Peeling paint chips can be an irresistible "snack" for children. Lead is a metal like mercury, aluminum, and others that have a tendency to accumulate in the body over time. These metals can be stored in the body until they eventually build to toxic levels. People often aren't aware of lead poisoning until this insidious accumulation process has begun to cause serious problems. Children are more susceptible to metals poisoning because toxic levels are reached more quickly in their smaller bodies.

In recent years, the Department of Housing and Urban Development (HUD) has helped focus attention on the lead-based paint issue. You may have seen ads in the real estate section of your paper for homes HUD has for sale. These are homes that have gone into default and are being resold by HUD under favorable prices and terms.

In these ads, HUD will identify homes containing lead-based paint with a "LBP" designation. This is an obvious indication of the high priority HUD is placing on the importance of warning homebuyers of the presence of lead in HUD homes for sale.

While having lead-based paints in your home is not exactly a positive selling point, it should also not come close to being a deal-killer on your sale.

A safe treatment of walls with lead-based paint is simple scraping and repainting. Lead is only harmful if it is ingested, and it is most easily ingested, especially by children, in the form of those tempting paint chips.

If your home has older lead-based paint walls, it shouldn't be a concern to you or your buyer, provided the painted surface is in good repair and not peeling. If you happen to run into buyers who are adamant in their objection to walls with lead-based paint, even if it is in good repair, this is one of the least expensive environmental concerns to rectify. It is better to foot the cost of painting a few interior walls than risk losing your sale.

Lead Pipes

The purity of America's drinking water is an issue that looms large on the horizon of our national priorities. Much of the concern about water revolves around industrial pollution and the depletion of natural supplies. But one of the most common threats to our drinking water is one of the oldest ones- from the lead in the pipes of our own homes.

Like asbestos and lead paint, lead pipes were a staple of American residential construction for many years. Even when copper pipes were used, lead still remained on the scene in the form of the lead-based solder used to connect copper pipes.

Lead is a soft metal which leaches into water more easily than many other metals. When water is at rest in a pipe with lead or leaded solder, lead leachate has a chance to accumulate its level of concentration. The leaching process is accelerated by warmer water.

Today plastic pipe is common for residential plumbing. But if you have an older home that you suspect may have lead pipes, don't panic. The first thing to do is find out if you have anything to worry about. Call your local water department- many of them offer free or low-cost water testing for customers with concerns about lead or other contaminants. If your water department doesn't provide this service, call a private lab capable of running such tests.

If the test is negative, any worries on behalf of you and your home's buyer are over. If lead is present in your water, you should deal with the problem pronto. Ask your water department what its policy on lead pipes is. In some cities,

lead contamination can be caused by a short pipe- sometimes called a "pigtail"—that connects the residence to the water main in the street. Since these connections were originally installed by the water department, they may absorb the cost of pigtail replacement.

If lead is present throughout the plumbing system of your home, you face a more complicated problem with the potential for high pipe replacement costs. You may want to consider installing high-quality filtration systems for all of your home's spigots in lieu of extensive pipe replacement. Today's heightened sensitivity to water purity has given rise to some excellent filtration systems capable of removing virtually all impurities, even chlorine.

You would be well advised to consult an attorney if you are selling a home with known lead contamination in the pipes, whether you install purification systems or not. Lead is a serious, high-profile contaminant; a heavy metal that must not be taken lightly.

When it comes to making any repair in order to sell your home, environmental or otherwise, it pays to stay calm and objective no matter how petty, alarmist, or insignificant the buyer's concerns may seem.

Above all, don't try to disguise flaws in your home just to save the cost of correcting them. That's one of the worst ways that a home seller can be penny wise and pound foolish. Your job isn't to win a battle of the egos with your buyer. Your job is to make the sale.

MATERIALS THAT COMMONLY CONTAIN ASBESTOS IN THE HOME

Roofing materials—roof felt and shingles
Window putty
Insulation—both blown in and batt varieties
Flooring—including tiles and undersheeting
Appliances—refrigerators, slow cookers, toasters, freezers, portable dishwashers, ovens, hair dryers, portable heaters
Built-in equipment—water heaters, dishwashers, range hoods, clothes driers
Interior coverings—acoustical tiles, sprayed on "popcorn" ceilings, some textured paints
Heating and piping systems—furnace and wall gaskets, duct inings, pipe insulation
Electrical materials—fuse and switch boxes, lamp sockets, electrical insulation, outlets

Automobiles—brake linings, gaskets, clutch materials
Miscellaneous—asbestos gloves, cat litter box materials, hot pads

ADDITIONAL INFORMATION SOURCES ON ASBESTOS

Consumer Product Safety Commission (CPSC) Hotline—for information about laboratories that do asbestos testing, and guidelines on asbestos removal and repair: 800-638-2772, or write the U.S. Consumer Product Safety Commission, Washington, D.C., 20207.

U.S. Environmental Protection Agency booklet "Guidance for Controlling Asbestos-Containing Materials in Buildings," Washington, D.C. Office of Toxic Substances, ESEPA EPA 560/5-05-084 (also known as the "Purple Book.")

U.S. Environmental Protection Agency (EPA) toll-free numbers:
800-334-8571, extension 6741—for names of labs qualified to test asbestos samples.

800-424-9065, for assistance to the general public regarding asbestos.

800-638-2772, for information regarding asbestos in homes and consumer products.

EPA REGIONAL ASBESTOS COORDINATORS

EPA Region 1
JFK Federal Building
Boston, MA 02203
(617) 223-0585

EPA Region 2
Woodbridge Avenue
Edison, NJ 08837
(201) 321-6668

EPA Region 3
Curtis Building
6th and Walnut Streets
Philadelphia, PA 19106
(215) 597-9859

EPA Region 4
345 Cortland St. N.E.
Atlanta, GA 30365
(404) 881-3864

EPA Region 5
230 S. Dearborn St.
Chicago, IL 60604
(312) 886-6003

EPA Region 6
First International Bldg.
1201 Elm St.
Dallas, TX 75270
(214) 767-2734

EPA Region 7
726 Minnesota Avenue
Kansas City, KS 66101
(913) 236-2835

EPA Region 8
One Denver Place
999 18th St., Suite 1300
Denver, CO 80202
(303) 293-1730

EPA Region 9
215 Fremont St.
San Francisco, CA 94105
(415) 974-8588

EPA Region 10
1200 6th Avenue
Seattle, WA 98101
(206) 442-2870

HOW TO AMERICA, INC.

GUIDELINES FOR SELECTING ASBESTOS CONTRACTORS

1. Require references from successfully completed asbestos projects, and check those references.
2. Require evidence of appropriate government licensing for asbestos contracting work.
3. Review contractor's written operating procedures for asbestos-related work; consult with your nearest EPA office to confirm that those procedures conform to accepted asbestos contracting practices.
4. Review list of special equipment that asbestos contractors should use, such as decontamination facilities, protective disposable clothing, air monitoring and control systems, etc. Make sure this equipment is in accordance with asbestos procedures as prescribed by your nearest EPA office.
5. Request disclosure of any asbestos projects prematurely terminated or unsuccessfully performed by the contractor, and any fines paid by the contractor to asbestos regulatory agencies or former clients related to breach of contract.

Final thoughts

HOME INSPECTION

This is a buyer's right that can make or break a sale over what are often trivial issues, so tiptoe carefully through this potential minefield.

For starters, you are now in a more advantageous position than you were the first time your buyers toured your house. They were prospects; now they are buyers. You know that they are now more interested in buying your home, because they have signed your earnest money agreement and given you a payment for at least 1% to 1 1/2% of the price of your home. Your buyers are serious, and they now have an emotional and financial investment in seeing themselves living in your home.

Home inspections can often turn out to be issues of pride. Sales have been lost because of petty disputes over nit-picky items. During the pivotal home inspection, you must be prepared for your buyers to be particular to the point of perfectionism. Ostensibly, the purpose of the home inspection is for the buyer's validation that repairs specified in the earnest money agreement have been satisfactorily made by the seller.

But some buyers may linger for hours, pad and pen in hand, writing up every paint scratch, driveway crack, loose tile, and even a soiled oven. The positive thing about this ritual is that , as long as your house is basically sound, the inspection will turn out to be nothing more than a "trivial pursuit." You should be as patient and understanding as possible during these sometimes marathon inspections. Listen, look, but don't get defensive or otherwise excited.

Buyers seem to have an instinctive urge to pore over every square foot of their home-to-be, like a mother hen's doting over a new nest, and rightfully so—its a major event in their lives. If you protest or act defensive, you may mortally alienate your buyers. Their final list of requests is likely to consist of items as inexpensive as they are simple to remedy. If your buyer's list of repairs does grow too long and unreasonable, remember that you are covered by the dollar limit of your liability for repairs specified in your earnest money agreement. Try to accommodate your buyer on their added-on repairs if at all reasonable. It may be a small price to pay to keep your sale intact.

A warning—if your home has a significant defect that is not detectable by means of normal inspection, you should disclose it to the buyer in writing. If such a defect is uncovered later without prior seller disclosure, the seller can be liable not only for necessary repairs of the deficiency, but for legal damages as well. The maxim of "let the buyer beware" only goes so far to protect sellers, especially in this liability-conscious era. Use your judgement, and when in doubt, rely on honesty.

Hopefully, your buyer will be satisfied with the results of their inspection, and not require a second inspection. If a second inspection does become necessary, it should be scheduled as soon as possible. If you are able to mutually agree that your home is in a condition acceptable to the buyer, you should add to the earnest money addendum that details repairs to be made, the statement "Buyers acknowledge that the above contingencies are satisfied." This statement should then be signed and dated by both you and the buyer immediately following the satisfactory inspection.

It is then your responsibility to forward copies of the amended and signed earnest money agreement and any addendums to your buyer's lender, escrow, and title company parties involved in processing your sale. At this point, your have soared over one of the last remaining hurdles…and one of the most serious potential stumbling blocks…in the race to the self-seller's winner's circle.

— — — — — — — — — — — — — — — —

NOTES:

CLOSING THE DEAL

As closing approaches, you will need to muster increasing reserves of resolve against overconfidence. Take for granted that the anxiety level of your buyers is likely to increase in direct proportion to the proximity of the approaching closing date. Communication is the key: continue to stay in constant touch with the buyer, buyer's lender, and escrow and title companies to make sure everything is progressing as planned.

Know what the closing process consists of in your area. In some states, closing occurs in the offices of the buyer's lender. Elsewhere, in an attorney's office. In many locales, closings are held at the title or escrow company.

You should be fully aware of all closing costs that will be required, and most importantly, you should take the time to sit down and review all of these costs with your buyer. There is nothing more disconcerting for a seller than the shocked face of an unprepared buyer at closing who is dumbfounded by the unexpected total of costs at closing.

These costs, which you should have already obtained an accurate estimate of from your escrow company, are summarized on the enclosed sample closing statement. The traditional responsibility for these individual costs is as follows:

Buyer	Seller	Split
Down payment	Property survey	Recording,
Loan fees	Title insurance	notary, and
Home inspection		other misc.
Appraisal		fees
Oil in tank		
Credit report		

The buyer and seller are each responsible for their respective attorneys' fees.

At closing, be prepared for a deluge of paperwork that you and your buyer will be expected to sign. A good closer should be willing to take the time to explain each cost to the satisfaction of both parties. Don't be afraid to ask questions, even if it considerably slows the pace of the closing session. You deserve to know the nature of everything you are paying for, and being paid.

After your sale is successfully closed, you have one last detail to attend to. After closing, your escrow company, attorney, lender, or other party responsible for closing should forward your transaction's documents to the county courthouse for the recording of those documents. This provides an official acknowledgement that the transfer of the ownership of your property has taken place according to the terms of your agreement.

After the closing has been completed, ask your closing agent how soon the documents will be delivered to the county seat for recording. Then, call the county recorder's office to make sure your recording took place as planned.

This is critical, because recording is the function that imparts full, final legality to your sale. Buyers or sellers who fail to ensure that their transaction is recorded do so at their peril, since the title to property is never transferred with certainty without the formal affirmation of recording. Technically, it is only after recording that your home is truly sold and your duties as a self-seller are complete. Except, of course, the most enjoyable task of the successful self-seller.

Deciding how you're going to spend all that money you just saved.

NOTES:

LAND SALES CONTRACTS

Many homes are sold without the benefit of conventional mortgage financing. One of the biggest reasons for that is that there are a lot of dependable home buyers out there who, for one reason or another, can't convince conventional lenders of their dependability as borrowers. Thanks to land sales contracts, these worthy buyers are still able to own a home, and most sellers are able to more easily sell their homes during tough financial markets.

Very simply, a land sales contract turns the seller into the buyer's lender. Instead of being paid off, or "cashed out" by a buyer's conventional home mortgage as the result of a sale, a seller may agree to finance, or "carry back" the balance of the sales price left over after the buyer's down payment.

Buyers seek sellers' contracts for several reasons; because they seek a lower down payment or interest rate than a regular lender would give them…because they want to avoid paying expensive loan fees…or because of credit histories that don't meet strict conventional standards.

Without question, contracts can be a good deal for both buyer and seller. For the buyer, it allows an avenue to home ownership that could otherwise be impossible. For the seller, it unquestionably broadens the field of prospective buyers and increases the likelihood of a faster sale. This is especially valuable in a down real estate market or a period of high mortgage interest rates (the two often occur simultaneously).

If you choose to go with a contract, you owe it to yourself to be as discriminating as a conventional lender would be in evaluating the reliability of your buyer. You should look carefully at the credit of contract buyers by ordering credit reports (you can request these from the same credit firms lenders use–they are listed in the phone book). You should also verify the buyer's employment status by contacting the employer directly. Confirm that the prospects for employment longevity are good. If they aren't, your buyer's ability to pay your monthly contract payments will be in jeopardy.

Sales contract regulations also vary from state to state, and you should definitely check with an attorney before finalizing your agreement.

Keep in mind that if you agree to provide such financing, you are truly doing the buyer a favor. It is not unusual for contract sellers to demand and receive compensation for their willingness to provide financing by setting the interest rates on their financing 1/2 to 1-1/2 percentage points or more above market interest rates. Where you set the interest rates on any financing you choose to carry is up to you, and it will again depend on your eagerness to accommodate a contract buyer in order to make a sale.

Second mortgages are usually structured like conventional home financing, with a 30-year term or "amortization period." Some sellers who don't want the funds being loaned to a buyer tied up for such a long period require that second mortgages be repaid long before the 30-year amortization period expires, such as at the 5-, 10- or 15-year mark. When these mutually agreed deadlines arrive, a buyer is obligated to pay off the second mortgage with what is called a "balloon payment;" or any payment that comes due prior to the end of a loan's amortization term.

For sellers who are willing to carry contracts on a home sale, but who want an even faster retrieval of their funds, there is another solution. Once a seller's contract is drawn and signed by the buyer and seller, it becomes a commodity with a value of its own that may be traded in the financial marketplace. A seller may take such a contract to a specialist who will translate the document's long-term value into immediate cash for the seller holding the contract. There is a catch, though, and that is that the seller will pay a penalty, or "discount" to the contract buyer in exchange for the advantage of receiving instant cash for long-term value.

The discount on such secondary contracts being sold varies according to the size, interest rate, and term of the contract in question. The older a contract, the less its discount will become when sold, since it accumulates credit worthiness as a track record of reliably made payments on the contract is established. This phenomenon is called "contract seasoning." If a contract holder can afford to wait a few years before selling the instrument, the discount will be steadily reduced with the passage of time and the seller will receive a higher value when the contract is finally sold.

HOW TO AMERICA, INC.

Contract selling is a common technique that shouldn't be intimidating, as long as you have competent legal advice for guidance. It can be a great redeemer in tough real estate markets. And, it should warrant special consideration for those sellers who are willing to convert their home equity into an investment that is paying high interest in the form of monthly payments. As long as your buyer is sound, you may find selling your home by contract one of the best investments you can make.

Remember a land sales contract should not cost you more than $350 in preparations.

NOTES:

HOW TO AMERICA, INC.

GLOSSARY OF COMMON REAL ESTATE WORDS AND THEIR DEFINITIONS

Abutting owner – the owner of a property that adjoins a public right of way.

Acceleration clause – a loan provision that allows a lender to demand full payment of a loan when a certain act occurs, such as failure to make regular payment, or the transfer of property ownership without the lender's consent.

Acceptance – the legal counterpart to "offer;" the two comprise a legal contract.

Acknowledgement – a written statement affirming and thereby executing a document. These are typically notarized to assume full legal credence.

Action to quiet title – an action to rectify any confusion about the true ownership of a property.

Addendum – a provision added to a document or agreement outside the main body of the document.

Adjustable mortgage loans or Adjustable rate mortgages (ARM's) – mortgage loans that start out with an interest rate significantly below the prevailing market rates for mortgage loans. Their interest rates are designed to move up or down over time, in response to key economic indicators to which individual loans such as these are tied.

Agency listing or agreement – also know as a "non-exclusive listing," this is a real estate agent's listing of a property that enables agent retention of a commission if a property is sold by any real estate agent, but not if the sale is made by the seller.

Agreement – the term doesn't carry the legal weight of the term "contract," but is generally regarded as the precursor to a formal contract either verbal or written.

Amendment – an alternation of a contract that does not change its basic purpose or spirit.

Amortization – the arrangement by which debt payments are made over time, which takes into account the ratio of interest and principal that changes as the loan matures.

Amortize – the process of debt reduction by a series of payments that are applied to both interest and principal.

Annual percentage rate (APR) – the true amount of interest paid on a debt. The government requires that lenders disclose the APR to borrowers.

Appraisal – a determination of a property's value based on objective property and overall market analysis.

Appreciation – the increase of a property's market value.

Appurtenance – an element of a property, either structural such as an outbuilding or legal such as an easement, that is transferable to any new owner of the property.

"As Is" condition – a status of property that does not infer a representation of quality, good or bad, by the seller at the time of sale.

Assessed value – value determined for tax purposes by government evaluators. This value may be significantly below true market value in many jurisdictions.

Assessment – this term has two meanings; the determination of a property's value to be used for tax purposes, and an obligation secured by the property typically for community-related improvements.

Backup offer – a second buyer who is in a position to replace a first buyer if a transaction fails to materialize.

Balloon payment – a payment or series of payments that are lump sums applied to the reduction of debt.

Breach of covenant – the violation of one or more stipulations of an agreement.

Broker - this term is often improperly applied to all real estate sales professionals, when in fact the qualification status of brokers is technically superior to that of a real estate agents.

Cancellation clause- a provision that specifies the conditions under which a buyer and seller would mutually agree to terminate an agreement.

Cashier's check- a check drawn on the account of a bank , rather than the account of one individual (such as your buyer). This type of draft is therefore a more reliable form of payment than a personal check.

Certificate of redemption- proof that a property has been re-purchased by the original owner after having been lost through default . Each state provides for a certain period of time following default during which an owner may buy back , or redeem , a property that has been lost .

Certificate of sale- an instrument given to the buyer of a property at a judicial sale following a default , which may not make the sale official until the period of redemption has elapsed .

Closing- the final execution of a sale which is affirmed by the recording of documents pertinent to the sale.

Cloud on title- an encumbrance against a property , either financial or physical , such as related to property boundaries.

Comparables- properties similar to one being sold which are used to help determine a seller's market price.

Condominium- a structure sub-divided into individual units which are individually owned, with additional land and building property which is commonly owned by the individual owners.

Contingency- an element of an agreement which must be satisfied before the total agreement can be consummated.

Counter offer- a response to an earlier offer that includes a modification of an agreement's terms.

Covenant- a legal term that refers to agreements or provisions of agreements.

Deed- a legal document used to convey title to a property , and a term relating also to documents of financing.

Deed of trust- a document whose purpose is similar to that of a mortgage, used in some states to secure a property for a lender until a loan is paid in full.

Equity- a property owner's net interest in a property; a property's value minus its encumbrances.

Escrow- a third party neutral to the interests of a buyer and seller who serves as an intermediary, who holds the property's deed, and executes the terms of a transaction based on instructions that are mutually agreed upon by buyer and seller.

Escrow instructions- directions issued to the neutral escrow agent that are agreed to by both buyer and seller.

Escrow agent or officer- a specialist in a given jurisdiction's escrow practices who serves as an objective intermediary between buyer and seller.

Fee simple- a term that basically is a synonym for ownership of property, that can be sold in any way and passed on to inheritors.

FHA (Federal Housing Administration)- a federal entity that acts as an insurer for loans made by private lenders, thus allowing loans to be made with terms more desirable to borrowers than other financing options.

General lien- an obligation secured by an entire property, as opposed to just a portion of the interest in a property.

Grantee- a person being granted something, such as a buyer of a property.

Grantor- a person granting something, such as the seller of a property.

Grantor- grantee index- the county documentation of all property ownership histories which is cross-indexed to allow property ownership to be readily determined using such factors as individual names, property addresses, tax identification numbers, etc.

Holding escrow- an escrow that endures for an extended period of time in order for the escrow agent to assure the performance of one or all parties in a transaction, as opposed to a typical escrow period which is in effect only long enough to execute the closing of a sale.

Home owners' association- a group of owners of homes in a given neighborhood or condominium development for the purpose of establishing and maintaining an agreed upon set of living standards applying to all affected property owners.

Joint tenancy- an equal right of ownership in a property that applies to two or more owners, and which calls for the rights of any deceased joint tenants to pass to the other tenants rather than heirs.

Lease- an agreement to rent space by a lessor (owner) to a lessee (tenant) in exchange for rent payment.

Legal title- technical ownership of a property, such as that by a lender holding the deed to an encumbered property, even though the property is owned and occupied by a private party.

Lien – an obligation against a property owner secured by the owner's property.

Market value approach- the determination of a property's value using a comparison of other similar properties in the area.

Mortgage broker- an intermediary who will research and arrange financing provided by a lender for a borrower seeking the most desirable loan terms.

Mortgage Insurance- assurance offered by an insuring entity that a lender's interests in a loan will be protected in the event a borrower defaults. Two of the largest providers of mortgage insurance are the Federal Housing Administration and Veterans Administration.

Plat map- a diagram specifying the location and dimensions of individual building lots and other real estate properties.

Plat book- a collection of plat maps for properties in an area.

Power of attorney- a legal device which allows one individual to represent another for the execution of legal acts. The power may be general, or all encompassing, or restricted to one particular act.

HOW TO AMERICA, INC.

Preliminary title report- summary of all interests involved in a property's ownership, that is issued prior to the completion of a sale or loan transaction.

Private mortgage insurance- a policy that protects the lender from default by a borrower, the premium for which is paid by the borrower.

Promissory note- often used to serve as earnest money for a home sale, the note is a representation to pay the amount of the note under the terms the note specifies.

Quitclaim deed- an instrument with which an interest in a property may be documented as discontinued.

Real estate or real property- anything that is attached to land, and attached to buildings on the land, as opposed to personal property, which is physically unattached and may be moved. (mobile homes, for example, are considered personal, not real property, because they are transportable.)

Reconveyance- an indication of the termination of a borrower's obligation to repay a debt secured for a lender, usually in the form of a trust deed. When the debt is paid, the title to the property is reconveyed to the owner.

Recordation- the legal acknowledgement of a transaction through the filing, or recording, of the transaction's documentation.

Secondary mortgage market- a market in which consummated loans are sold to investors, usually at a discount, to generate additional funds for lenders to issue new loans.

Second mortgage- a loan that is subordinate to a property's first mortgage. A property may have several mortgages against it, each ranked in order of priority.

Security land contract – also called an installment land contract, this is a hybrid of a land contract and a deed of trust which excludes a lender's right to call a loan due on sale, but preserves a trust deed's aspects regarding foreclosure.

"Subject to" clause – a provision in a deed which makes the responsibility for any loan deficiency that of the original maker of the mortgage.

Tenancy in common – a mutual ownership of a property by two or more persons whose interests in the property, in the event of any tenant in common's death, passes to legal heirs rather than the other tenants in common.

Title insurance – insurance issued to protect against any losses resulting from title encumbrances.

Title search – the process by which a property's title history is reviewed to reveal all parties who have an interest in the property and the nature and degree of their interest.

Trust account – an account supervised by parties neutral to a transaction in which funds are held prior to closing.

Warranty deed – a deed that includes a warranty of a property's title that is assured by the issuer, or grantor, of the deed. This is a duplication of the protection provided by title insurance.

How To Buy Foreclosed Real Estate

by Theodore J. Dallow

Whether you're searching for the "dream" deal on a property you intend to live in, or trying to find a highly profitable investment, Theodore Dallow is the man to listen to. His easy-to-understand guide shows even people without any real estate background how to profitably buy foreclosed properties. *How to Buy Foreclosed Real Estate for a Fraction of Its Value* will answer any and all of your questions.

Trade paperback, 1-55850-026-X, $8.95
5 ½" x 8 ½", 96 pages

Available wherever books are sold.

Credit Approved

by Kevin Pilot

The credit system can be complex, confusing, and often completely arbitrary. *Credit Approved* explains how to re-establish credit when you have a bad credit history, and how to establish credit if you have no credit history whatsoever. Kevin Pilot's book also explains how to correct credit bureau errors that can have a devastating impact on your future.

Trade paperback, 1-55850-111-8, $5.95
5 ½" x 8 ½", 144 pages

Available wherever books are sold.

Live Debt- Free

by Ted Carroll

Live Debt-Free is a simple, legal, and thoroughly commonsense approach to personal debt. It shows how you can save a tremendous amount of interest by staggering important purchases such as houses and automobiles. Purchase agreements for these items are usually stacked in the bank's favor; early on, you pay enormous amounts of interest, and very little on principal. *Live Debt-Free* shows how you can reverse the cycle.

Trade paperback, 1-55850-044-8, $7.95
5 ¾" x 8 ¾", 160 pages

Available wherever books are sold.